THE SECRET LIFE OF A FUNDRAISER

Wasif Hani

INDIA • SINGAPORE • MALAYSIA

ISBN
Paperback 979-8-89906-648-1
Hardcase 979-8-89961-610-5

Dear God,

Sorry for being a constant complaint box, but I trust You'll set things right in the end, You will yeah?

Thank You for my child, the little soul who reminded me of the strengths I had long forgotten.

Thank You for the timing. I didn't always agree with it, but now I see that everything happened exactly when it was meant to. Your clock never misses a beat, even when mine felt stuck.

And if it's not too much to ask, could You use me as a channel to reach those who feel the pull to do good? To those who want to leave this world just a little better than they found it, may my journey speak to them. May they keep learning, keep inspiring, and above all, keep spreading the love.

And finally, heartfelt gratitude to mom, dad, and better half for their patience, their love, and for tolerating the big shift. Am sorry I hurt them through this process. Please forgive me.

With Faith,

– Wasif Hani

Contents

Foreword

Stepped into the unknown. No plan. No blueprint. No research. Just a strange pull and willingness to surrender to something bigger. Call it madness or faith. Maybe it was both. Not chasing strategy but chasing meaning.

At some point, I wondered what if a celebrity or an industry expert wrote this foreword. It would sound impressive. Feel official. But then, like most of life itself, I ended up doing it myself. And honestly, I wouldn't have it any other way. I might as well write this piece too.

There were countless days I found myself drifting into another life, far removed from the one I knew. I imagined myself behind the wheel of a black G-Wagon, moving through the world with quiet authority. My expression was unreadable, a poker face, eyes squinting, daring anyone to challenge it. A cigar burned slowly between my fingers, while heavy hip-hop pulsed through the air, a soundtrack that warned the world not to come too close. That version of me was power personified with calm, command, and control.

But that was just a fantasy.

In reality, I still take the Mumbai trains to work. Shoulder to shoulder with strangers. Wrapped in the noise, the movement, the messy poetry of everyday life. No tinted windows to shield me. No curated playlist to set the mood. Just the raw rhythm of the grind, steady and unrelenting. And maybe that is exactly where I am meant to be. Not soaring above it all but rooted in the heart of it. Not to be admired from a distance but to be present, to feel, to understand. Not to conquer but to contribute. Made perhaps not for escape or spectacle but for something quieter. Something real. A different kind of purpose.

The Secret Life of a Fundraiser isn't a manual. It doesn't offer formulas or foolproof hacks. It's a window into a life lived behind the curtain. A life of silent battles, invisible labour, and the relentless pursuit of something meaningful. It's about holding on when it's easier to let go. About building relationships when nothing guarantees a return.

I wrote this book in solitude. Quietly. Without noise, without applause. Just me and the weight of what needed to be said. And now, I place it gently in your hands. For those walking their own paths not defined by market trends, who've felt invisible while trying to make a difference. You are seen. You matter. This is for you.

Come as you are.

Let's begin. Welcome to the Secret Life!

Preface

This book was born out of curiosity, frustration, and an overwhelming urge to share the untold side of fundraising for non-profits. It had been sitting in my head for years. At one point, I even thought, *Maybe I should do a stand-up comedy show on this!* Because, let's be honest, fundraising for non-profits has enough plot twists, awkward encounters, and unexpected punchlines to fill an entire set. But that never happened (probably because I never made the effort to actually achieve it).

Along the way, I found myself training students, new recruits, and even various Non-Government Organisations on the subject of fundraising. And while that was fulfilling, I had this nagging feeling that this story needed to go beyond my little circle, beyond the organisation I work for, beyond the social sector, or maybe even beyond borders, kind of like Elvis Presley, who always dreamt of performing internationally but never could as he was trapped by circumstances beyond his control, despite the global appeal of his music.

Many moons later came the moment that pushed me over the edge. I was at a conference, watching speakers from around the world sharing insights on various subjects, and I couldn't help but sulk. *Hey, man! I should be up there, talking about fundraising for non-profits!* The frustration was real.

But instead of just sulking, I did the next best thing and spoke to my good mate, Mr Pete Miller. After many conversations, in the final moments before he embarked on a long journey to explore and capture Nepal, the decision was made: I should write this book!

When I first stepped into the world of fundraising, I had no prior experience in the field, no network to lean on, and was in fact new to the country with absolutely no idea what to expect. What I did have was an instinct, a belief that I could make an impact by bringing people and resources together for a cause. What followed was a ride of unexpected lessons, rejections that tested my patience, and victories that felt like tiny miracles.

Fundraising is often seen as simply asking for money, for support, for a moment of someone's time. But what many don't realise is that it's just as much about *giving*. Giving effort where results aren't guaranteed, giving hope when the odds seem impossible, and giving trust in relationships that take time to build. It is both an art and a science, and more often than not, a test of patience and persistence.

Although it's a world where rejection is a daily reality, so is the possibility of hearing that one "Yes" that changes everything.

To anyone standing at a career crossroads, feeling uncertain, seeking purpose, or simply craving a meaningful change, know this: you don't always need to have it all figured out. My journey into fundraising began with no roadmap, no connections, and no clear plan. Yet it led me to work that truly matters. Whether you are drawn to the social sector, client relationships, or just want to do something that makes a difference, sometimes the most unexpected paths lead us exactly where we are meant to be.

So here it is, '*The Secret Life of a Fundraiser*'. A journey into the unseen, the unexpected, and the extraordinary. Wishing you well, dear reader.

Loads of love,

– Wasif Hani

Acknowledgements

This book is the result of a deeply personal journey. Written, rewritten, and stitched together through sheer self-effort.

I chose, quite deliberately, to walk this path mostly on my own. Not out of pride, but because I wanted to test my resolve without the comfort of a crowd that often celebrates your wins but vanishes in your lows. I sought the stillness, the rituals, the mental loops, and the quiet struggles that taught me lessons no external guidance ever could.

I didn't speak of this pursuit to many. In fact, to hardly anyone. Just like the title, I wanted this journey to remain quiet. Lived in spirit, felt in solitude.

It was messy. Unpredictable. Lonely at times. But strangely enough, it was also liberating.

To my family, thank you for holding space for my madness, for trusting the process even when it made no sense from the outside.

To the few who offered encouragement, your words, gestures, or quiet presence nudged me forward more than you'll ever know.

Mr Pete Miller, stay with me. I need you in those moments when belief feels distant.

To the non-profit fundraising world, with all your chaos and beauty, you gave me stories worth sharing.

This one is for the silent strugglers. The lone rangers. The ones chasing meaning behind closed doors.

A New Beginning

After 30 long years in Dubai, a city that shaped me, embraced me, and became the backdrop of my life, I found myself on a flight back to Mumbai. My wife sat beside me, and in our arms, we cradled our one-year-old child. It was a journey I never thought I would take in reverse, a chapter I never imagined closing, a farewell I wasn't ready to write.

Even now, I can still feel the weight of that final night. We were at a quiet restaurant, sharing what was meant to be our last dinner in the city. But somewhere between the food and the farewells, the emotions caught up with me. I broke down right there in the middle of the hall, my heart too full and my eyes too heavy.

The waiter stood still, unsure of what had just unfolded. I reached out, shook his hand, and through tears, whispered a prayer to him: May God help you achieve whatever you seek. His confusion met my gratitude, and in that moment, our brief exchange became something sacred, a silent goodbye to a city I had loved, lived, and finally left behind.

Looking back, my life in Dubai had always followed a structured path. My personal school life was anything but ordinary. My mother was a teacher at my school, and my father was the principal of another school. There was no room for error. I had to be the good boy of the class, the one who lived up to the expectations set before me.

That discipline and structure carried over into my professional life. I spent a decade in banking, split between two major institutions, navigating the fast-paced world of frontline operations, the strategic depths of the mid-office, and the meticulous precision of the back office. It was a career built on numbers, systems, processes, and relationships. And yet, somewhere along the way, a different calling had begun to take shape, one that no spreadsheet or risk analysis could have prepared me for.

The decision to return to India was made. Not easy, but made. There were professional and personal undercurrents that made it complex, perhaps a story best left for another day. But what mattered in that moment was the step I had taken. I enrolled at a premier institute in Mumbai for a course in the social sector, an 18-month whirlwind of learning, unlearning, and immersing myself in a world far removed from the one I had known. Branch banking, treasury markets, and payment investigations were replaced by conversations on impact, policy, and social change.

As the course came to an end, I found myself at yet another crossroads, this time in search of a job. Stepping into an entirely new landscape, I began a relentless cycle of interviews with various NGOs, each encounter exposing me to a different dimension of India's social sector, its causes, its challenges, and its people. Some organisations accepted me, others rejected me, and in a few cases, I walked away myself, unsure if I was the right fit.

The process was humbling, eye-opening and at times frustrating. Unlike my previous career, where experience and expertise often determined the next step, this sector had a different rhythm. Passion mattered, but so did persistence. Connections played a role, but so did sheer luck.

Upon my return to India, I met many well-established professionals who questioned my choice. "Why the social sector? There's no money in that!" But I didn't budge. I simply replied, "Yeah? I'll still do it."

This was a phase with no concrete plan but just a willingness to take life one day at a time and the faith that somehow, things would fall into place.

And then, the day arrived. There was that one interview where we both selected each other. It was the perfect intersection of ambition and opportunity. With that, I stepped into my new role as a fundraiser. It felt like standing before a blank canvas, paintbrush in hand, ready to create something from scratch. The possibilities were endless. The challenge was exhilarating. And oh yes, the pocket was empty too. My savings had all but washed away in this unusual pursuit of meaning.

Fundraising is a world few truly understand. Beyond the polished pitches and glossy reports lies a reality of persistence, rejection, strategy, and sheer human connection. More than ever, the world needs people who can bridge the gap between resources and impact, between those who wish to give and those who need support.

This book is a window into that journey, a rare glimpse into The Secret Life of a Fundraiser. It unravels the unseen struggles, the relationships built and broken, the high-stakes pitches, the bizarre encounters, and the relentless pursuit of that one "Yes" amid a sea of "Nos." Whether you're an aspiring fundraiser, a donor, or simply someone curious about what happens behind the scenes of the social sector, this book will take you on a journey filled with lessons, surprises, and stories that will hopefully make you think and maybe even smile.

It's time, dear reader. Let's begin.

DONATE

Chapter 1

Lone Ranger's Hunt

The Leap of Faith

Starting over is never easy. Starting over in a completely new sector, in a country that felt more alien than familiar, was terrifying in a way I hadn't known before. I wasn't just switching careers; I was shedding an entire identity. From corporate boardrooms to non-profit corridors, I was now a stranger in my own homeland, armed with little more than reckless hope and a blank Excel sheet.

For over a decade, I had built a solid foundation in the banking world. I had learned to interpret numbers, navigate the maker and checker maze, process applications, and manage client portfolios with precision. I knew how to thrive under the unforgiving gaze of auditors and had developed the subtle art of dealing with people from every walk of life. Those years taught me cultural nuance, discipline, and resilience. And yes, there were times it threw me hard onto the floor too many times.

But none of that prepared me for what came next.

Suddenly, I found myself at the bottom of the non-profit pyramid, looking up at the Everest of fundraising with no map, no mentor, and no margin for error. Just blind optimism and a quiet, stubborn voice in my head that kept repeating, "you can't fail." Because failure meant becoming that story people would whisper about, "Wasif acha ladka tha, par kya kare" *(Wasif was a nice boy, but what to do?)*.

The first six months felt like running on fumes, powered by faith, chai, and sheer willpower. There was no Plan B. It was all or nothing. I had to make this work or go down trying.

My task was clear: build a list of potential donors from scratch. And my resources were practically non-existent.

I had no connections in the sector and no powerful relatives to call in favours. It was just me, Google, and a wildly idealistic dream. After 30 years in Dubai, I had returned to Mumbai, thinking I could brute force my way into a new purpose. I refused to lean on old contacts. Maybe it was pride. Maybe it was ego. Or maybe I simply needed to know if I could build something on my own. Alone. Like a lone wolf, except without a pack or even survival instincts.

In hindsight, maybe not the smartest choice. Would I recommend it to anyone else? Absolutely not. But at the time, it felt like the only way.

And then came the moments of doubt. The heavy ones. The kind where you miss the simplest comfort of having a friend by your side. I often caught myself wishing Navin was there, a close friend, an anchor through countless misfit moments we had shared back in Dubai. He would have looked at me, grinned, and said, "Eda moonay, you'll get it done," in that calm, knowing, witty way of his.

But Navin wasn't there. Neither was Sanker, another brother from my inner circle of sanity. They were back in their worlds, and I was here, raw, alone, and scrambling.

Ironically, I had just completed an eighteen-month course in social development where I had written essay after essay about the transformative power of empathy. I wrote about how it was the lifeblood of non-profits, the holy grail of human connection. I truly believed in it.

And then reality showed up. Not with a polite knock but like a high-speed crash in one of those chaotic movie chase scenes, with metal, glass, and dreams flying everywhere.

Out in the field, empathy wasn't exactly in the air. If anything, it was missing in action. If I had to write that essay again, I wouldn't write about how empathy holds the sector together. I'd write about how shockingly hard it is to find when you need it most.

I had to stop looking for understanding and start focusing on what I could bring to the table. I had to earn my place, not expect an invitation.

So, I did what any lost soul with a laptop would do.

Hey Google,

Find me CSR heads. Show me donor databases. Give me something to hold onto.

There was no secret playbook. But if one existed, I was determined to find it, even if it meant clicking through the thousandth search result at two in the morning, hoping for one correct email address and one working phone number.

It was the start of something messy, maddening, and magical in its own twisted way.

The Blank Excel Nightmare

And so, it begins. Excel is open, staring back at me like an unimpressed teacher waiting for my homework. The cursor blinked mockingly, as if tapping its foot in impatience. My Excel sheet? A barren wasteland, an endless desert of empty cells, where hopes of finding contacts went to die. No leads, no names, just me and the crushing realisation that I was going to take a while doing this.

I had started this sheet with the best of intentions, convinced that if I meticulously listed out potential corporate donors, the money would soon follow. That optimism lasted all of three days. My list remained pathetically empty. I had to do something and had to do it fast. But, I needed that kick as the mojo was going down.

Wake-Up Call

Amidst my thought process on how to start and where to start, my mind kept drifting back to a conversation that quietly, yet profoundly, changed my perspective.

During my course's research phase, I had one of these deep-dive sessions with cancer survivors and caregivers. Here, I met a woman whose story didn't just move me; it kind of shook me. Her husband was battling cancer.

Her son, a survivor himself, was their only earning member. Their entire family, which included parents, siblings, and in-laws, squeezed into a single rented room where personal space was a distant dream, and privacy was a concept that belonged to another world. Comfort, certainty, even the ability to exhale without worry - these were luxuries they couldn't afford.

Yet, she wasn't bitter. She wasn't angry. She wasn't even asking for help.

"Main poora din daudti rehti hoon," she said with a tired yet unwavering smile. *I run around the whole day.* And I believed her. Because in her world, there was no space for self-pity, no room for breakdowns. Survival wasn't a choice; it was the only option.

Her words lingered in my mind long after the conversation ended. Here I was, frustrated over a blank spreadsheet of where to begin, and this real superwoman had every reason to break down but was still moving forward, still fighting, still standing.

And then, like a slap of perspective, it hit me. If she wasn't giving up, then what right did I have to?

I had a job. An opportunity. A mission, so to speak. It was time to stop overthinking and start doing, man!

The Location Hack: From Nowhere to Somewhere

Enter: Google Maps.

One evening, armed with determination (and a mug of overly sweet chai), I zoomed in on corporate hubs near my home and office. Pharma companies, manufacturing giants, educational institutions, heck, even a textile firm that, as I later discovered, had surprisingly deep CSR pockets.

I clicked on company names, scoured 'About Us' pages, and like a detective piecing together clues, I compiled whatever scraps of information I could find. It was like digital treasure hunting, a CSR manager's name, an email, or, if the stars truly aligned, a working phone number. Other times, I got that personal favourite, that dreaded info@company.com.

But I kept going.

And from there I started one by one. The Excel spreadsheet began to have a few rows and columns. What was once a barren landscape started to bloom with some names, numbers, and job titles. Each new entry felt like a small step for fundraising, a giant leap for my kind!

I had something now.

A *chota* (small) list. A direction. A starting point.

Beyond the Location: The Google Deep Dive

I had crafted twenty entries now to start, but I needed more. A lot more. What if I was missing the real giants? The big players who could make a game-changing difference for my non-profit?

So, I did what any resourceful fundraiser would do – I let Google take the wheel.

I started typing: *Top 10 CSR projects in India. Top 20 companies with the best CSR programmes. Top 50 biggest corporate donors.*

Google did not disappoint. I found rankings, articles, research papers, and even award lists. Suddenly, I wasn't just scraping together random corporate emails; I was curating a hit list of the country's most influential CSR champions.

One search led to another, one article to five more tabs, and before I knew it, I had fallen into a digital rabbit hole. My Excel sheet grew. Twenty turned into 30. Then 40. Then 60.

I sat back, staring at the once-empty sheet now brimming with names, numbers and email addresses.

This was it.

I had built my own database from scratch.

Now it was time to pick up the phone and start making calls.

The Great Indian Dial-A-Thon

Here we are - the list of 'potential leads.' Chances. Opportunities. Doors. Now, all I had to do was start knocking those doors, one by one.

But in my mind, this wasn't just knocking. This was the Wild Wild West, and I was about to step into a high-stakes cowboy showdown. Where it's always a hot sunny afternoon in a deep desert town. The street dead silent. A lone haystack tumbling by, as if it, too, wanted no part of what was about to go down. Saloon doors creaked. Somewhere, a harmonica played a single, ominous note. Townsfolk peeked through wooden shutters, clutching their hats and muttering, *"Poor fool doesn't stand a chance."*

It was just me... and the empty, merciless leads before me. Would I strike gold, or would these numbers send me face-first into the dirt? The cursor blinked at me like a cowboy's twitchy trigger finger. Any moment now, one of us was going to make a move.

Oh, Clint Eastwood, thanks for the memories. Now, let's see if I can survive this duel.

I straightened my back, took a deep breath and transformed my humble little desk into a one-man call centre.

Here we dial, here we call!

I dial my first number.

Disconnected.

Ok, let's go for the second?

Wrong number.

The third?

"Sir, this is a restaurant."

Huh! The glamorous life of a fundraiser has just begun aye?

Most numbers led to dead ends, some connected to businesses that had long vanished, and a few reached people who had absolutely no idea what CSR even was.

But then, finally, a breakthrough.

The phone rang. Someone answered. My heart raced. This was it! I straightened my posture (as if they could see me) and launched into my pitch.

Silence.

Then came the response:

"Madam seat pe nahi hai." (*Madam is not in her seat.*)

I blinked. That was... unexpected. But okay, maybe I'll call back Madam later?

"Alright," I said, "when would be a good time to call?"

More silence.

And that's when I realised that I had just pitched my entire case to the office boy.

I could have laughed. I could have cried. Instead, I took a deep breath and dialled the next number.

And the next.

And the next.

Kept going because somewhere in that frustrating list was the call that would lead to the meeting that would open the first real door. I hoped.

The LinkedIn Gamble

Desperation breeds creativity. And at this point, I needed a miracle.

Enter: LinkedIn.

During my conversations at work, I came up with a decent idea - what if I just started congratulating people here?

Not just anyone, though. Award winners. The kind of professionals featured in 'Top 50 Leaders' lists or honoured with industry accolades. Those who held real decision-making power.

So, I crafted the simplest message:

"Congratulations on your well-deserved award! Wishing you continued success."

No pitches. No requests. Just pure, feel-good flattery.

I carefully crafted my messages and lined up my target 15 LinkedIn connections who, at first glance, looked like they might just loosen their purse strings. I won't lie, I judged them by their profile pictures, their job titles, and that gut feeling of *hmm… this person looks like someone who will give.* With a deep breath and a silent prayer to the fundraising gods, I hit send. One by one, the messages flew into the digital abyss.

Now, all I could do was wait. Refresh. Stare at the screen. Refresh again. Any moment now, a response would come in.

Nothing happened that day. "Let's check again tomorrow," I told myself. "We did well today," I added, like a coach consoling a low-scoring boxer after round one. I shut my laptop and headed home.

24 hours later.

A notification on LinkedIn. A message. Whoa!

There it was. A reply from the gentleman himself. My heart pounded like a drumroll before a grand reveal, but I had to play it cool. *Deep breath. No sudden movements.*

I clicked open and read his kind message.

In response, I typed back, *"Thank you so much! Appreciate your kind words, Sir!"* Trying to sound composed while I was internally doing cartwheels.

Ping! Another reply. This time, he wasn't just being polite – he was interested. He spoke about the social investments his company makes across various causes.

That's when it hit me. *I see it. HALLELUJAH!*

The stars were aligning; the fundraising gods were smiling. I seized the moment.

"Let's connect and explore if our organisations can work together!" I pitched, subtly wiping imaginary sweat from my forehead.

From a cold LinkedIn message to a direct conversation with an industry leader in under 24 hours. This is the beginning of something huge, or was I about to be left in limbo? There was only one way to find out.

The conversation flowed. A little back and forth on social contributions, his passion for CSR, and the kind of impact he wanted to make. It felt like God himself was laying the bricks on this path. And then the moment arrived.

"Let's take this forward."

Boom. Just like that, the gentleman vanished.

Was he an angel? A fundraising mirage? No, he was actually the MD of the company. But before I could process the win, his secretary swooped in. And now, *she* was running the show.

Calls. Meetings. More calls. Due diligence. Site visits. I was deep in the trenches. Like a cowboy back for a second duel at high noon or a boxer who had been knocked down in round one but was now back on his feet, swinging harder than ever.

And then, the world stopped.

COVID hit. Yeah! Beat that!

Everything came crashing down. Deals? Frozen. Projects? Stalled. Rumours of clients and other donors swirled like a bad soap opera.

"The agreement lapsed."

"They pulled out."

"How could they withdraw?"

Such bad news spread faster than a baby boomer's WhatsApp forward. It wasn't pretty. And there I was, hands clasped, eyes to the heavens, *pleading* with the Almighty for just *one* shot.

Some days passed. And then on a Monday, at exactly 8:30 pm, my phone rang.

The secretary's number flashed on the screen.

This is it. Whatever happens, happens, I told myself. Either way, it'll be fine. Right?

I picked up.

She answers, *"Hogaya"*.

I froze. Hogaya means *Done?* as in… *done done?* Or *not done?*

She sighed, probably sensing my brain short-circuiting.

"Oho, approved!"

I stood still for a moment, letting her words sink in. My heart pounded as the realisation hit me that this was THE MOMENT.

Took a deep breath and said, *"Thank you, Ma'am. This is amazing news for all of us."*

I looked around the room, my mind racing. My eyes landed on my kids' toy set, scattered across the floor. And there it was, a long cricket bat.

Without thinking, I picked it up. The smooth handle felt firm in my grip. I stood in front of the mirror and raised it high in the air, like a batsman who had just hit a match-winning six.

Because in that moment you bet I had!

Still buzzing with excitement, I grabbed my phone and messaged my CEO. A few seconds later, his email was sent across to the board members with the subject: *"New Donor Alert."*

And just like that, I had arrived.

Truth Bytes

The Call That Changed My Perspective

I had been part of this fundraising forum for a short while, mostly missing lectures thanks to a sprained neck, and when I did show up, I was just there to nod painfully at fancy jargon as if I understood any of it.

Then, one day, luck struck! I won a golden ticket to a one-on-one, ten-minute video call with one of India's top fundraising heads from a leading pan-India NGO.

Excited? Absolutely.

Nervous? Nah, not much.

I had exactly 600 seconds to pick the brain of a fundraising genius, but I chose to listen instead.

Here's what happened:

As the call connected, there she was: well-poised, confident, radiating the kind of energy that could probably convince a rock to donate to a water conservation project.

After the pleasantries, I asked, "What's the most important thing I should know about fundraising?"

She leaned in slightly and said, "There are two sides to a coin in the NGO sector."

I nodded, pretending I knew where this was going.

"On one side," she continued, "are the programmes which include the field teams, the daily warriors, the operations folks who keep the NGO running."

I nodded again. Made perfect sense.

Then, she paused, making a slightly dramatic effect, and asked, "And do you know what's on the other side?"

I blurted out, "Impact? Awareness? Administration?"

She shook her head with a knowing smile. "No. It's fundraising!"

Mic drop moment.

She continued, "Everything else, all the other functions, exist to support these two functions. No fundraising? No programmes. No programmes? No NGO."

I could almost hear my non-fundraising colleagues gasping in collective shock. I pictured someone from Finance clutching their spreadsheets like a life raft, HR furiously shaking their heads in denial, and Communications whispering in despair, "But… but storytelling matters too!"

Too late, players. The truth bomb had been dropped.

Was it a bit uncomfortable to digest? Maybe. But was it absolutely true? You decide.

But for myself, I had a realisation of the importance of Fundraising. Many don't call this out, but I guess this was the new reality settling in within me, and it will continue forever.

That ten-minute call reshaped how I saw fundraising. It wasn't just about asking for money. It was about ensuring that the mission, the heart and soul of the NGO, kept beating. And in this process, it will ruffle a few feathers along the way. You just have to find your space on the table.

Chapter 2

The Social Sector Landscape in India

To be clear, I'm no expert on the social sector. I don't have groundbreaking theories, policy jargon, or a 15-point framework to solve all the world's problems, especially the Indian NGO landscape. What I do have is a front-row seat to the chaos. Over the years, I've seen, heard, and observed enough to pen this book. And because I'm feeling generous (and maybe a little mischievous), I'm going to share a slice of that with you.

I'll admit, I steer clear and stay far away from panel discussions and grand conferences where people in well-tailored blazers and Banarasi sarees discuss how to transform the social sector. I opt out of attending not because I'm busy solving world hunger, but because these events can sometimes feel like an advanced-level buzzword competition. There's always someone championing "scalable impact," another highlighting the perils of "donor fatigue," and, inevitably, someone who manages to weave the word "synergy" into every other sentence. No disrespect, but hey, I'm the audience who's listening.

I could be one of those people. I could wear a crisp blazer, nod thoughtfully, and say things like, "We must reimagine the future of social impact." But I don't. Partly because I'm not sure what to say, and partly because no one invites me to these discussions anyway. Which, frankly, works out just fine. I prefer being on the ground where the real action is, chasing donors, navigating bureaucratic mazes, and occasionally wondering if Excel sheets were invented as a form of medieval torture. And yes, I take gut punches on a weekly basis, chasing departments, prepping reports, following up like a maniac, just to make sure everything lands neatly in someone's inbox before the deadline gods get angry.

Back to these conferences. I usually sit quietly, watching the wild world of PR unfold before my eyes. High-fives fly through the air like celebratory fireworks, and people talk to people who talk to other people in an endless chain of rapid-fire pitches. The whole scene buzzes with the energy of professional matchmaking. It's networking on steroids. And how can we forget the laughs? They're so damn loud and constant, I sometimes find myself thinking, *Man, why can't I have a life that happy?!*

Meanwhile, I sit back and let the show play out. I should be up and about, thrusting my visiting card into the hands of the who's who, but I wait. Not a great habit, I know, but that's me. I tell myself I'm adopting a strategic, mysterious allure. Let the universe work its magic. Surely, it will deliver the right person to me at the right time. Yeah, some wishful thinking!

From my seat in the last row, I witness it all. Enthusiastic handshakes that linger a bit too long, exaggerated nods meant to signal deep interest, and the occasional overzealous networker who pounces on anyone who even resembles a decision-maker. But me? I'm just waiting for my moment, hoping destiny taps me on the shoulder.

And then, like clockwork, it happens.

A gentle tap on my shoulder jolts me out of my observational trance. My heart skips a beat. *This is it,* I think. The universe is finally delivering my big break. I turn around with the hopeful glimmer of someone who believes their future is about to change.

A man stands there, smiling brightly. *This is my moment,* I tell myself. I rise from my seat, smoothing my clothes and preparing my dazzling introduction. Before I can speak, he leans in and says, "Hey, could you do me a favour?"

I nod eagerly, ready to make an impression. Anything for a potential donor connection, yeah?

"Can you take a picture of us?" he asks, shoving his phone into my hand.

I blink. My grand vision of a million-dollar partnership crumbles in real time. I glance over to see two beaming faces, his "new colleagues," standing arm in arm, practically glowing with the joy of freshly minted professional synergy.

Their Relationship status: *Established.*

My Relationship status: *Complicated and when on earth is it going to begin?!*

I force a smile, swallow my pride, and take the picture because that's what you do when the universe serves you humble pie on a silver platter. I make sure to capture their best angles (if I'm doing this, I'm doing it right), hand the phone back, and sink back into my chair with a sigh.

Another successful connection, not mine, of course, but someone's. Ah, the glamorous life of a fundraiser. One photo-op at a time.

Real Talk: The Complex Web

Way beneath the surface of these conferences and networking events lies the reality of India's social sector. It is a vast and evolving ecosystem where public, private, and civil society organisations intersect to address some of the country's most pressing challenges. From grassroots movements to large-scale corporate philanthropy, the sector operates at the intersection of poverty alleviation, healthcare, education, environmental sustainability, social justice, and much more.

If you're imagining fundraisers running around with donation buckets, think again. This is a world where spreadsheets, strategy decks, endless grant application forms, and the occasional existential crisis reign supreme.

Picture this: the Indian social sector is like a big, chaotic family reunion where there is a cake to be cut. During the party, everyone talks at once and no one agrees on who should go ahead and cut the cake. Some people claim they brought the cake, so they deserve special attention. At the centre of this noisy gathering are the tireless relatives who actually roll up their sleeves and get things done while everyone else argues about who gets the biggest slice.

The metaphor humbly compares the Indian social sector to a chaotic family reunion. Here's a breakdown:

- *The 'Cake' symbolises resources and credit*:

  Everyone wants a piece of the cake, which represents funding, recognition, or influence. Some organisations claim they brought the cake, implying they were the first or most important contributors.

- *The 'Noise' reflects diverse and conflicting voices*:

  Like a loud family party where everyone talks at once, the social sector is full of varied opinions, agendas, and approaches. There's rarely a common consensus on how things should be done, which creates both a vibrant mix of ideas and a surge of energy and potential solutions.

- *NGOs are the doers*:

  While others argue or claim credit, NGOs are the 'tireless relatives' who get things done, working on the ground and delivering impact.

Now let's not forget, credit must also be given to the broader ecosystem beyond NGOs, which includes government bodies, philanthropic foundations, Corporate Social Responsibility (CSR) initiatives, and many other grassroots movements. These players, each with their unique strengths, often collaborate to amplify impact and drive systemic change. While NGOs may be on the frontlines, these other entities provide crucial policy support, funding, and large-scale infrastructure that make sustainable progress possible.

The Indian social sector is a complex web of idealists, realists, bureaucrats, and the occasional opportunist. For every genuine, ground-level warrior making an impact, there is also a maze of red tape, endless donor reports, and a game of funding musical chairs where someone is always left standing. And just like any big family, there are internal dramas, turf wars, philosophical debates about the 'right' way to do good, and a generous helping of gossip about who's really making a difference and who's just here for the photo ops.

At its best, the social sector fills gaps between the government and private sector, providing essential services to millions who would otherwise be left behind. At its messiest, it is a scramble of competing interests, opaque processes, and a never-ending hustle to keep the lights on. And yet, despite the chaos, it somehow works out! Because behind every jargon and grant proposal are real people fighting real battles, hoping to make even the smallest dent in the world's problems.

Poverty in India: Beyond the Numbers, Inside the Struggle

Behind the polished panels and the corporate buzzwords lies the stark reality that fuels the entire social sector - its poverty. It is the unrelenting backdrop against which all of us in the sector operate. For every grant proposal, strategy deck, and networking event, there are millions of lives grappling with daily struggles that no PowerPoint slide can fully capture.

Poverty in India is not just a statistic. It is a lived experience, a daily negotiation for survival. To truly understand the social sector, you must understand the weight of what we are working against.

Despite being one of the world's fastest-growing economies, a significant portion of the Indian population continues to struggle with poverty. Millions of people live below the poverty line, grappling with inadequate access to basic necessities such as food, clean water, healthcare, and education.

One of the defining characteristics of poverty in India is its multidimensional nature. It extends beyond just a lack of income to include limited access to essential services, social exclusion, and vulnerability to economic shocks. Rural areas bear the brunt of poverty, with agrarian distress and lack of infrastructure contributing to widespread hardship. Urban poverty, a concept I recently came to understand, manifests in the form of sprawling slums, informal employment, inadequate housing, and poor representation.

Structural inequalities further exacerbate the situation. Caste, gender, and regional disparities create additional barriers for marginalised communities. Women and children, in particular, are disproportionately affected by poverty. Malnutrition, child labour, and low literacy rates remain pressing concerns, especially in rural areas and underserved urban pockets. In all this, a major portion of the middle class takes a heavy beating too. Caught between rising living costs and limited social welfare benefits, they often struggle to maintain financial stability while being overlooked in poverty alleviation programmes.

The fight against poverty in India is ongoing, requiring a multi-faceted approach that combines policy reform, community engagement, and sustainable development efforts. For fundraisers working within this landscape, understanding the nuanced realities of poverty is crucial. It is not enough to write compelling proposals; you need to feel the weight of the problems you are trying to solve. Because behind every report, every pitch, and every donor call is a human story that is raw, urgent, and waiting to be heard.

An Outsider's First Encounter with the Social Sector

If you thought navigating the Indian social sector was complex from the outside, stepping into it as a newcomer is an entirely different ballgame. Imagine walking into a new school mid-year where everyone already knows the rules, the lingo, and the best spot to sit during lunch. You, on the other hand, are still trying to figure out if you need permission to use the bathroom. Conversations swirl around you with phrases like "CSR compliance," "impact metrics," and "Pan-India scalability."

If your idea of social work was handing out food packets, welcome to the real deal! Here you're more likely to hand out decks than dal.

The reactions you get when you tell people you are entering the social sector are just as entertaining. Some folks tilt their heads and ask, "Social sector? What will you eat?",

"Oh dear! What will you do? You need something to fall back on." As if you have traded a steady paycheck for a lifetime supply of free goodwill. Others assume you have taken a vow of poverty, destined to survive on idealism and *vada pav* at every field visit. While their concern is touching, the reality is far more nuanced and far more interesting.

Gone are the days when working in the social sector meant donning a khadi kurta and carrying a jhola, that iconic cloth bag, while quoting Gandhi. Today's social sector is a buzzing professional ecosystem where MBAs, policy analysts, data scientists, and communications strategists work shoulder to shoulder with grassroots activists. Whether you are a fundraiser, CHRO, CFO, CEO, or any functional head in between, there is a seat for you at the table, assuming you can keep up with the acronyms and survive the avalanche of emails. And of course, get the work done professionally.

Don't be fooled, this isn't a hobby club. Fundraising isn't just about telling heartwarming stories anymore. It's about crunching numbers, digging into market research, and crafting proposals sharp enough to impress a room full of eagle-eyed donors. And if you think you can slide by with good intentions and a charming smile, think again. Behind the scenes, there is a performance matrix silently judging you, and yes, your survival may just depend on how well you can wrestle with Excel.

Sure, the salaries may not match the corporate world just yet, but the trade-off is worth it *if* you're willing to look for it. You tackle real problems, witness your work creating tangible change, and on the best days, you feel like you're helping to make the world a little less broken. Plus, you'll gather enough wild stories to be the most interesting person at any dinner party. Not a bad deal, right? But if you're here for the money, don't compare it to the corporate world. This side of the fence plays by different rules.

If you are comparing your paycheck or the watch you wear to your friends in consulting or tech-related jobs, prepare for some humbling moments. But here is a truth worth remembering. While someone else may be flaunting a limited-edition timepiece, you are out here helping to change lives. And honestly, there is no luxury brand that beats the feeling of saving a child's future or ensuring a family has access to clean drinking water. So, take it easy on yourself because *purpose* outlasts *possessions*.

If you are planning to jump into the social sector, here are a few survival tips to keep your sanity intact.

First, learn the players. Figure out who is who among NGOs, CSR folks, and foundations, and how to speak their language without sounding like a robot.

Second, get comfortable with chaos. Plans will change, emails will be ignored, and meetings will spiral into philosophical debates. Adapt, improvise, and keep moving.

Third, balance heart and hustle. Passion is great, but it won't pay your bills. Strategic thinking, patience, and persistence will. And let's be honest, you can't cash in good vibes at the grocery store. Don't be like me, diving headfirst without a backup plan. But if you're the kind who loves to go all in, just remember this: big risks can lead to big rewards, or a spectacular crash. Either way, it's one hell of a ride.

Fourth, celebrate small wins. Change in this sector takes years, sometimes decades. Every tiny "yes," no matter how small, deserves a celebration.

Finally, keep your sense of humour; a little laughter goes a long way.

At the end of the day, the social sector is not for the faint-hearted. It is messy, unpredictable, and occasionally feels like a never-ending reality show. But if you stick around long enough, you will experience moments of real magic. These are the moments no corporate bonus can match because when you play even a small role in improving someone's life, every sleepless night, every chaotic meeting, and every Excel-induced meltdown suddenly feels worth it. The thrill of seeing a big cheque come through because of your work from start to finish is a feeling like no other.

And who knows, if you stick around long enough, you might just become that person at the conference casually dropping words like "synergy" while keeping a perfectly straight face.

Truth Bytes

The Mysterious Fundraising Trade Offer

Back in my early fundraising days, on a random Monday morning, my phone rings. It's an unknown number. I hesitate, then reluctantly pick up.

Me: Hello?

New Girl (excited, slightly nervous): Hi! OMG, is this *Wasif Hani*? I just started fundraising and have heard so much about you! *(She doesn't know I'm new to this function myself.)* Have been following your LinkedIn posts regularly.

Me (cautious): Uh... thanks? Who's this?

New Girl (speed-talking): Oh! Sorry! I'm new to this whole fundraising thing, just trying to, you know, learn the *tricks of the trade.* So… small request… could you, um, share some donor emails?

Me (blinking):…Did you just ask me for donor data over a random phone call?

New Girl (giggling nervously): Haha, when *you* say it, it sounds so bad! But no, you can think of it like an *exchange!* You help me, I help you… you know?

Me (suspicious):…Help me *how*?

New Girl (whispering): You know…aa… *you know.*

Me (frowning): No, I don't know.

New Girl (groaning): Noooo! I mean I'll… I'll help you out! Give you *something*! You know!

Me (deadpan): At this point, I *really* don't know.

New Girl (desperate): UGH. Fine. Just *tell me* what you want!

Me: Ma'am, please send an email. I'll seek an approval from my CEO.

And we hang up the phone.

Moral of the story: When in doubt, "Please send an email" is the best exit strategy.

Chapter 3

Many Faces of Giving

—— •❧• ——

The dust of uncertainty had begun to settle, giving way to a quiet clarity. I was finally finding my rhythm. Like a newcomer at an exclusive club, I wasn't making loud introductions, shaking hands, or diving into the centre of the action. I wasn't the party starter, nor the life of the party. I stood at the edges, watching the world play its cards, letting the rhythm of this new space reveal itself to me.

Perhaps I had always been this way, a silent observer, absorbing details that others brushed past. And now, in the world of fundraising, that instinct only sharpened. What once felt like chaos was starting to show patterns, hidden beneath the surface of generosity and governed by unspoken rules.

There were three major kinds of donors, and I was beginning to see them clearly. On paper, the categories were simple. But in reality, they were as layered as the people behind them, each with their own motivations, pressures, and unsaid protocols.

But before I could master the categories, I had to learn the terrain. I had stepped into the game. Now, it was time to understand how it was played.

With time, the patterns emerged. Fundraising wasn't just a chaotic marketplace of giving. It had its own structure, its own silent logic. And yes, the law, above all, is the one that could send shivers down any NGO's spine.

Every interaction, every closed door, every unexpected opportunity revealed something new. And at the heart of it all were the donors, the ones who made everything possible, yet remained the most unpredictable players in this space.

Broadly, they fall into three categories:

1. **Corporates**

2. **Foundations**

3. **Retail Donors** – This includes both high-net-worth individuals and the humble givers of the mass market.

At first glance, these seem straightforward. But dig a little deeper and you'll find a world of nuance. Each donor is shaped by a unique mix of motivations, constraints, and decision-making rituals. No two donors are alike, and while social media memes poke fun at their quirks, the truth is every donor is a story, sometimes a full-blown case study.

Let's start with corporate donors.

Unlike individuals who give based on emotion or personal connection, corporate giving is bound by structure. Behind each donation is a CSR team guided by internal mandates and rigid policies, policies that are often not just difficult to bend but nearly impossible to touch.

But here's the twist. CSR laws are as unpredictable as stock markets, political shifts, and, yes, human nature.

India, for instance, was the first country to mandate CSR under the Companies Act 2013. The European Union leans towards sustainability reporting, emphasising accountability for environmental and social impact. And the U.S., in true free-market style, trusts corporate self-regulation, though Fortune 500s often lead the way in philanthropic efforts.

Which brings me to a quick disclaimer.

CSR laws are subject to change. Just like the weather, your mood, and yes... even your underwear (hopefully daily).

Governments love tweaking regulations. So before making any big moves, check with your legal advisor, an official source, or if all else fails, a psychic. They might have better luck predicting policy changes anyway.

And in India, oh boy, we love our psychics, don't we?

So, stay updated. Stay legal. And most importantly, stay fresh with your compliances.

I'm not taking responsibility if you follow outdated laws and end up explaining things to tax officials, investors, or your accountant, who suddenly starts Googling 'how to disappear without a trace'.

Let's go!

1. Corporates

These Corporate Social Responsibility (CSR) rules vary across countries. Here's a comparison of CSR regulations in different countries, handpicked randomly:

India (Mandatory CSR)

* **Law:** Companies Act, 2013 (Section 135)

* **Requirement:** Companies with a net worth of ₹500 crore, turnover of ₹1,000 crore, or net profit of ₹5 crore must spend at least 2% of their average net profits from the last three years on CSR activities.

* **Enforcement:** Non-compliance leads to penalties, and the unspent amount must be transferred to government-specified funds.

United Kingdom (Voluntary but Strongly Encouraged)

* **Law:** UK Companies Act 2006 (Section 172) & Modern Slavery Act 2015

* **Requirement:** No mandatory spending, but companies must report on CSR activities, including human rights, environmental impacts, and anti-slavery efforts.

* **Enforcement:** Non-compliance can affect reputation, shareholder trust, and access to government contracts.

United States (Voluntary)

* **Law:** No federal mandate; follows SEC reporting guidelines.

* **Requirement:** Companies are encouraged to disclose CSR initiatives voluntarily, especially related to ESG (Environmental, Social, Governance) performance.

* **Enforcement:** Public perception, investor pressure, and state-level regulations (e.g., California's transparency laws) drive CSR efforts.

European Union (Mandatory ESG Reporting)

* **Law:** Corporate Sustainability Reporting Directive (CSRD), Non-Financial Reporting Directive (NFRD)

* **Requirement:** Large companies must disclose their impact on environmental, social, and governance (ESG) factors.

* **Enforcement:** Companies face fines or reputational risks for failing to meet reporting requirements.

China (Partially Mandatory)

* **Law:** Company Law & Environmental Protection Laws

* **Requirement:** Large state-owned enterprises (SOEs) are required to disclose CSR efforts, while private firms are encouraged to follow ESG standards.

* **Enforcement:** Government regulations focus on environmental responsibility and labour laws.

Brazil (Voluntary but Encouraged)

* **Law:** Brazilian Corporate Law & Environmental Regulations

* **Requirement:** Companies are encouraged to contribute to CSR initiatives, especially related to Amazon rainforest protection, labour rights, and social development.

* **Enforcement:** Public and investor pressure influence CSR compliance.

France (Mandatory ESG Reporting)

* **Law:** French Duty of Vigilance Law (2017)

- **Requirement:** Large companies must monitor their supply chains, human rights, and environmental impact.

- **Enforcement:** Companies face lawsuits if they fail to comply.

Germany (Mandatory for Large Companies)

- **Law:** German Supply Chain Due Diligence Act (2023)

- **Requirement:** Companies must ensure ethical supply chains and report on social and environmental responsibility.

- **Enforcement:** Fines and legal consequences for violations.

Australia (Voluntary but Encouraged)

- **Law:** Modern Slavery Act 2018

- **Requirement:** Large companies must report on efforts to combat forced labour and human rights abuses.

- **Enforcement:** Non-compliance can lead to reputational damage.

Let's talk about the regions where I grew up and which are quickly catching up to better standards and best practices - CSR regulations in the Middle East!

They vary by country, with some nations having mandatory requirements, especially for ESG (Environmental, Social, Governance) reporting, while others follow voluntary guidelines influenced by Islamic finance principles and government-led sustainability initiatives.

CSR Regulations in Middle Eastern Countries:

United Arab Emirates (UAE) - Partially Mandatory

- **Law:** CSR Law (2018) & Securities and Commodities Authority (SCA) Regulations

- **Requirement:**
  - Large companies are encouraged to allocate 1% of annual profits to CSR activities.
  - Publicly listed companies must disclose sustainability and ESG initiatives.
  - Focus on sustainability, labour rights, and community development.

- **Enforcement:**
  - Non-compliance does not lead to direct penalties but may affect public image and investor relations.

Saudi Arabia - Voluntary but Strongly Encouraged

- **Law:** Saudi Vision 2030 & Capital Market Authority (CMA) ESG Guidelines

- **Requirement:**
  - No mandatory CSR spending, but companies are encouraged to align with Vision 2030 goals.
  - Listed companies must report on ESG performance (social responsibility, environmental impact).
  - Emphasis on Islamic finance ethics, philanthropy (Zakat), and sustainability.

- **Enforcement:**
  - Public and investor scrutiny drive compliance rather than legal penalties.

Qatar - Mandatory for Some Sectors

- **Law:** Corporate Governance Code & Qatar Stock Exchange ESG Guidelines
- **Requirement:**
  - Qatar Stock Exchange-listed companies must report on ESG and CSR efforts.
  - Financial and energy sectors have mandatory CSR reporting due to their impact on sustainability.
  - Focus on education, environmental conservation, and economic diversification.
- **Enforcement:**
  - Companies failing to report may face investor backlash and reputational risks.

Kuwait - Voluntary but Influenced by Islamic Finance

- **Law:** Kuwait CSR Reporting Framework (Financial Sector)
- **Requirement:**
  - No fixed CSR spending, but listed companies are encouraged to disclose social and environmental efforts.
  - Financial institutions must integrate Islamic finance principles into their CSR initiatives.

- Focus on philanthropy, environmental responsibility, and corporate ethics.

- **Enforcement:**

  - CSR performance affects investor confidence and government relations.

Oman - ESG Reporting Becoming More Common

- **Law:** Oman Vision 2040 & Corporate Governance Code

- **Requirement:**

  - No mandatory CSR spending, but companies are encouraged to report ESG efforts.

  - State-owned enterprises and major industries (oil, gas, banking) must disclose sustainability efforts.

- **Enforcement:**

  - Government and public expectations drive CSR participation.

Bahrain – Mandatory for the Financial Sector

- **Law:** Central Bank of Bahrain (CBB) CSR Guidelines

- **Requirement:**

  - Financial institutions must report on CSR and ESG activities.

  - Companies are encouraged to support social welfare, environmental sustainability, and economic growth.

- **Enforcement:**
  - Financial regulators monitor compliance, and companies risk reputational damage for failing to meet standards.

And alas, how can we forget our African ancestors?

South Africa - Mandatory for Certain Companies

- **Law:** Companies Act & King IV Report on Corporate Governance

- **Requirement:**
  - Johannesburg Stock Exchange (JSE)-listed companies must integrate CSR into governance and report on sustainability efforts.
  - Businesses must engage in Broad-Based Black Economic Empowerment (B-BBEE), ensuring fair employment and economic participation for historically disadvantaged groups.

- **Enforcement:**
  - Non-compliance affects business licences, government contracts, and reputation.

Nigeria - Partially Mandatory for Some Sectors

- **Law:** Nigerian Sustainable Banking Principles (NSBP) & Companies and Allied Matters Act

- **Requirement:**
  - Banks and financial institutions must follow CSR guidelines related to social responsibility and environmental impact.

- Oil and gas companies must invest in community development under Nigeria's Local Content Laws.

- **Enforcement:**

  - Companies risk government penalties and community backlash if they neglect CSR obligations.

Kenya - Voluntary but Encouraged

- **Law:** Companies Act & Capital Markets Authority (CMA) ESG Guidelines

- **Requirement:**

  - Publicly listed companies must disclose CSR and ESG efforts.

  - CSR in Kenya often focuses on education, health, and environmental conservation.

- **Enforcement:**

  - Government and public pressure drive CSR compliance.

Ghana - Mandatory for the Extractive Industry

- **Law:** Ghana Mining Regulations & Petroleum Local Content Law

- **Requirement:**

  - Mining and oil companies must contribute to local development (e.g., infrastructure, healthcare, education).

  - Companies must follow Environmental and Social Governance (ESG) reporting.

- **Enforcement:**
  - Companies that fail CSR obligations face fines, licence suspensions, and community protests.

Egypt - Voluntary but Influenced by Islamic Ethics

- **Law:** Egyptian Stock Exchange ESG Guidelines
- **Requirement:**
  - Companies are encouraged to integrate CSR, especially in environmental sustainability and social welfare.
  - Islamic finance principles, including Zakat (charitable giving), influence CSR activities.
- **Enforcement:**
  - No strict penalties, but strong government encouragement and investor expectations.

Phew! That's enough of our world tour through corporate policies. Let's return to the real heart of this chapter.

So, what drives these donors? And how do their decisions shape philanthropy? Let's dive deeper.

Within these laws exist the employees, the unsung heroes of corporate philanthropy, who must navigate the rigid frameworks of CSR policies. Their role isn't just about signing off donations; it's about balancing compliance, impact, and corporate interests within a structured system.

Let's zoom in on India, where yours truly, the author of this book, has not only firsthand experience but also a few battle scars to prove it! Here, CSR is not just a choice but a legal mandate. The 2% CSR rule under the Companies Act of 2013 has transformed corporate giving into a strategic, policy-driven exercise. Yet, behind the official reports and compliance checklists lie the real stories, the challenges, the loopholes, and the human element of corporate giving.

So, who are the different breeds that exist in CSR? What happens behind these closed doors? Let's uncover.

CSR, when done right, is powerful. But when done for PR, it's just philanthropy's glitzy, less effective cousin. As you navigate this world, keep your eyes open for who's truly in it for impact and who's just in it for the LinkedIn clout.

The Many Shades of Corporate Donors

(A light-hearted take. Hey, no offence intended!)

Corporate donors come in all shapes and sizes. Some are here to change the world; others just want a good photo op. But hey, a donation is a donation! So, let's have some fun and break down the many species of corporate givers:

The Spotlight Philanthropist

Always camera-ready, they arrive at donation drives in spotless white shirts, distributing aid with one hand and posing for a DSLR with the other. For them, philanthropy isn't just about impact, it's about visibility. After all, if there's no press release, did the donation even happen?

The Branding Enthusiast

For these donors, charity and corporate branding go hand in hand. They're happy to fund a school, just as long as the entrance gate bears their signage. A hospital wing? Of course, but with the logo.

The Quiet Contributor

A rare but admirable breed. They fund projects, expect no banners in return, and brace yourself, sometimes don't even post about it on LinkedIn. You won't find them on stage at a ribbon-cutting ceremony, but you will find them making real change happen.

The Impact Analyst

These donors thrive on spreadsheets the way plants need sunlight. If it can be charted, graphed, colour-coded, or buried in a 15-slide deck, they're all in. Throw in reports like 'Impact Metrics', 'LFA' and 'Monthly Utilisation Table', ideally wrapped in a glossy PDF with at least three pie charts, then my friend, you've basically written their love letter.

The Legacy Builders

They don't just donate; they invest. Their projects, whether schools, hospitals, or skill centres, are designed to last long after the CSR budget cycle ends. Their focus is sustainability, with a little self-congratulation. Let's say, many congratulations!

The Invisible Changemakers

These are the quiet doers who focus on impact over applause. They fund large-scale initiatives without turning every effort into a branding exercise. If you see well-maintained public infrastructure without a giant corporate banner, you've likely found one of these silent champions.

The Employee-Driven CSR Warriors

Some organisations believe that real impact happens when employees actively participate. They create programmes where employees contribute their time and skills to meaningful causes. When CSR becomes part of a company's culture, it starts being a core value along with a solid KPI to be ticked.

The Sustainable Investors

These companies focus on social impact that aligns with long-term environmental and economic sustainability. Their initiatives aim to empower communities, drive economic growth, and support ecological balance, not just for today, but for the future. Don't mess with them; they partner with the government. *Smile and wave, people! Just smile and wave!*

Now let's take a look at the foundations.

2. Foundations *(let's talk about the ones in India)*

India has a diverse landscape of foundations, each working tirelessly to tackle society's toughest challenges. These organisations, whether family-run or independently established, serve as the financial backbone for many impactful initiatives. But getting them on board? Well, that's a different story altogether. If you think it's as simple as sending a proposal and getting a cheque, think again. It's more like auditioning for a reality show where the judges grill you on every minute detail before giving a thumbs-up.

Types of Foundations in India

1. **Family Foundations**: Think of them as the cool uncles and aunts of philanthropy. They have money, they care about causes, but they like things done their way, sometimes with more heart than logic.

2. **Independent Philanthropic Foundations**: These are the serious players with a long-term vision. They do their homework, have deep pockets, and will ask you every possible question under the sun before making a decision.

3. **Community-Based Foundations**: They focus on hyper-local impact and often operate with a hands-on approach. If your project aligns with their vision, they'll be your biggest cheerleaders.

The Onboarding Nightmare

You know how they say, "Good things take time"? Well, securing funding from foundations in India is proof of that. It's a test match, not a T20. Be prepared for months of back-and-forth discussions, emails, site visits, budget justifications, and an interrogation that might make you question why you started in the first place.

Larger foundations, in particular, will grill you harder than a street vendor making tandoori chicken. They'll scrutinise every detail, demanding to know exactly how many rupees go into a child's meal, how many hours a teacher spends in the classroom, and whether your team's office chai is being funded by their grant (spoiler: it better not be!).

If you're the one managing donor relationships, congratulations! You've just signed up to be part diplomat, part saint, and full-time reality show contestant. The prize? Funding. The obstacles? Endless follow-ups, budget edits at midnight, donors who vanish like your weekend plans, and programme associates grilling you like it's their PhD viva. Buckle up, legend!

Expect:

- The same question being asked five different ways, just to make sure you're not bluffing.

- Requests for documents you didn't know existed (and might have to create overnight!).

- Random "urgent" calls when you least expect them, probably when you're just about to bite into your lunch or just about to go to the loo for your morning ritual. Yup, try holding 'that' to answer some cost per beneficiary questions!

The golden rule? **Never lose your cool.** No matter how frustrating it gets, keep your responses clear, polite, and patient. Treat it like a never-ending oral exam where hopefully the examiner will get tired and let you pass.

The Reward: A Loyal Foundation Partner

Once you survive the onboarding battle, it's all smooth sailing, well, mostly. Until they meet you again for the year-end review. And yes, grill you again!

Foundations that invest in you after this rigorous process tend to stay for the long haul. They'll fund you year after year, support your scaling efforts, and even advocate for your work to other funders.

However, that doesn't mean you can rest easy. You need to:

- **Deliver on promises:** If you said you'd educate 500 kids, don't show up with 450 and a nervous smile. And if you promised to spend ` 1 crore, don't pull a disappearing act at ` 83 lakhs. Either hit the number, go beyond, or (pro tip) agree *in advance* that a 10% wiggle room is allowed. Because explaining why you underspent after the fact is like telling your boss you "almost" came to work on time. Cute, but nope.

- **Be transparent**: Share financial reports, impact metrics, and success stories. Keep them in the loop so they never feel out of touch.

- **Exceed expectations:** When possible, over-deliver. This keeps your foundation partners excited and willing to extend their support. Yup legit!

The game is worth it, and it's a must-do!

Yes, the process is long, tedious, and at times excruciating. But in the end, having a strong foundation partner is like having a mentor who believes in you and fuels your journey. If you can survive the onboarding gauntlet with patience, a rock-solid impact plan, and number crunching where even a NASA scientist gives you a standing ovation, then you'll not only secure funding but also a loyal supporter for years to come.

So, take a deep breath, grab that cup of chai (again, not funded by the grant), and get ready for the ride!

3. Individual Giving - *HNIs and Mass-Market Donors*

Philanthropy is no longer just about foundations and Corporate Social Responsibility (CSR) initiatives; individual giving has emerged as a significant force driving social change. Broadly, individual givers can be categorised into two distinct groups: the High Net-Worth Individuals (HNIs) and the mass-market donors. While both are essential for the non-profit ecosystem, their approaches, expectations, and impact differ vastly.

The Titans of Giving: HNIs

HNIs have deep pockets and the ability to match the contributions made by corporate giants and large foundations. Their generosity is substantial, and so is the process of securing their support. To paraphrase an old adage, Jesus said, 'Keep your friends close, but your enemies closer.' The fundraiser, however, says, 'Keep your corporates close, but your HNIs closer.'

Why? Because courting an HNI is both an art and a science. Unlike a mass-market donor who may contribute out of pure altruism, an HNI's philanthropy often comes with expectations. The cause, delivery of results, the change, impact metrics, and, in a few cases, the brand alignment, as well as a well-documented paper trail.

However, in the modern fundraising landscape, there's a twist. The direct access that NGOs once had to HNIs has been obstructed by the rise of aggregators. These intermediaries function like an immigration department standing between non-profits and the donors, meticulously filtering access. They refer to the HNIs as "clients" and won't reveal their identities until a later stage of evaluation. Till then, all an NGO can do is speak to the aggregator, keep the conversation going, and perhaps wish, pray, and cross every finger available.

Once an NGO does make it through the gates, the process is not over. Quarterly reports, extensive due diligence, and the same old drill of paperwork become a recurring cycle. The funds come with restrictions, and every rupee needs to be justified.

But if you ever find an HNI who doesn't ask for reports, congratulations! You've just hit the philanthropic jackpot! That's rarer than spotting a unicorn popping *pani puri* at Juhu Beach while debating the *theory of change* with you!

The Humble Champions: Mass-Market Donors

On the other side of the spectrum, we have the mass-market donors. These are individuals who give out of a deep connection to the cause, a simple desire to help, or even for tax-saving benefits. Their contributions may not be as hefty as those of an HNI, but their collective impact is profound.

The beauty of mass-market donations lies in their flexibility. Unlike funds from HNIs, which are often earmarked for specific projects, mass-market donations are usually unrestricted, allowing NGOs to allocate them where they are needed most, be it filling critical gaps, covering operational costs, or responding to emergencies.

Additionally, these donors serve as powerful ambassadors for a cause. Whether through word of mouth, social media advocacy, or community engagement, they spread awareness in ways that money alone cannot achieve. Their enthusiasm fuels movements, inspires others to give, and amplifies impact beyond monetary contributions.

Striking a Balance

Both HNIs and mass-market donors play indispensable roles in the philanthropic ecosystem. HNIs bring financial heft and long-term support but demand rigorous accountability. And yes, there are those few gold coins that won't.

Mass-market donors, on the other hand, contribute not just funds but also passion, advocacy and flexibility.

For NGOs, the challenge is to navigate both worlds effectively by building meaningful relationships with HNIs while also cultivating a broad base of grassroots supporters.

At the end of the day, philanthropy is not just about money; it's about connection, trust, and a shared vision. Whether it's an HNI signing a big cheque or an everyday giver making a small contribution, every act of giving fuels the mission and brings us one step closer to a better world.

Lessons learnt

One Size Fits None

Donors may be categorised into corporates, foundations, and individuals, but their policies and motivations vary wildly. Some give because they care, some because they have to, and some because their marketing team insists on a giant logo.

If you think one strategy will work for all, congratulations, you've unlocked Level 1 of Fundraising Fantasy!

Corporate Philanthropy

Corporate giving is part heart, part strategy, part compliance, part paperwork, and part paranoia because the government is watching you. In some countries, CSR is a legal requirement. But whether they're in it for compliance, branding, or genuine impact, one thing's for sure: your proposal will go through a bunch of review rounds.

Some companies give quietly, some loudly, and some ensure their logo is bigger than the project itself. Understanding who loves the limelight and who prefers working in the shadows is key to building strong partnerships. Either way, expect emails and meetings, and just when you think it's done, a quick impact assessment with HD pics will be needed.

The Great Foundation Treasure Hunt

Applying for foundation grants requires patience and persistence. The process is long, the paperwork is extensive, and just when you think you've answered all possible questions, there's one more questionnaire. But once you're in, foundations can be some of the most stable partners. As long as you deliver on impact and numbers in the budget, you are in it to win it.

Individuals: The Unsung Heroes of Giving

High Net-Worth Individuals (HNIs) are generous but hard to access. Think of them as the VIP concert tickets that sell out before you even know they exist. Meanwhile, mass-market donors may not give millions, but their collective impact is game-changing. The trick? Engaging them *without* flooding their inbox with donation requests.

Universal Currency of Trust, aka Transparency

Whether it's a corporate, a foundation, or an individual donor, one golden rule applies – be clear, be accountable, and never, ever fudge the numbers. Transparency isn't just a virtue; it's the glue that holds donor relationships together. Regular updates, honest reporting, and tangible impact will keep them engaged. And if you can exceed expectations? Well, that's how you turn one-time donors into lifelong champions.

When the hill gets steep, climb.

When you're tossed into the deep, swim.

When it rains on your plans, dance.

If you can see it, you can build it.

If you can dream it, you can fundraise it.

No storm, spreadsheet or stubborn stakeholder can stop a determined fundraiser on a mission.

Keep going. Keep grooving. You've got this, player!

Truth Bytes

Fundraising or Investment Banking?

Interviewer: We need a Senior Fundraising Manager. USD 7.5 million to be raised annually. Can you deliver?

Me: USD 7.5 million? In a year? I bring experience and skills like...

Interviewer: Who's in your portfolio? Ticket sizes?

Me: My... what? You mean donors?

Interviewer: Can you name a few donors, and can you transfer your portfolio here if you are with us?

Me: Huh? Does this happen in this sector?

Interviewer: How much of the funds can you immediately mobilise?

Me: <blank silence>

Interviewer: So, no guarantees? Hmmm

Me: It's *fund*raising, right? Not *fund*-taking.

Interviewer: We'll be in touch.

Me: Just to confirm… this *is* a non-profit, right?

Interviewer: *Already left the Zoom call.*

Moral of the story: Fundraising is about passion, relationships, and impact… unless you're in the wrong room, where it suddenly feels like Wall Street!

Chapter 4

Art and Science of Proposals

One evening, just as the day was winding down, a message arrived from the CEO with an urgent request. A CSR had opened an unexpected funding window, and a proposal needed to be submitted by morning.

My heart sank. It was already past 7 pm. I had no template ready, no prior donor engagement with this corporate, and barely any time to research their priorities. But I knew one thing: if we missed this window, there would be no second chance.

I pulled up my existing proposals, borrowed elements from different documents, and pieced together a fresh one. The framework took shape, the narrative started flowing, and within some time, a draft was ready. But there was one missing piece - the numbers. The finance team didn't start until 10 a.m., and that meant an agonising wait.

The next morning, I kept glancing at the clock, willing it to hit 10 am. The moment it struck, I grabbed my phone and called finance, fingers crossed that they would prioritise my request. "I need the budget breakdown ASAP," I pleaded.

They got to work. The next two hours were a flurry of back-and-forth messages, clarifications, and last-minute tweaks. By noon, I had the final numbers, plugged them in, and sent the proposal to my CEO.

The donor acknowledged receipt. By the end of the week, we got the call. Our proposal had been shortlisted. The funding wasn't guaranteed yet, but we had made it to the next round. And that would not have happened if we had hesitated or waited for a "perfect" draft.

Never assume you'll have ample time to craft the perfect proposal. Opportunities can arise at any moment, and when they do, speed matters. A proposal isn't just a document; it's your ticket to potential funding. The more prepared you are, the quicker you can respond, and the higher your chances of success.

Always have a few templates ready. Keep key sections pre-drafted. And when the call comes, don't overthink but simply start writing and fill in your budget. Because in fundraising, the best proposal isn't always the most polished one; it's the one that reaches the donor's desk on time.

Why Do Proposals Matter?

Proposals are the bridge between a fundraiser's passion and a donor's commitment. They translate dreams into numbers, emotions into impact statements, and aspirations into structured plans. A well-crafted proposal does not just seek funding; it inspires confidence. It reassures donors that their money will be well-utilised, aligns their frequency with yours, and helps them come close to their informed decision.

The proposal is your story, your handshake, your first impression, and your credibility check, all wrapped in one singular document.

What Makes a Proposal Effective?

Many fundraisers believe that a proposal is just a standard document with a request for funding. But it is much more than that. It is a conversation on paper. It needs to answer five key questions. Please allow the guest lecturer in me to give in...

1. What?

What is your NGO trying to achieve? What problem are you solving? This should be clear, concise, and backed by data. Avoid jargon and speak in a way that a donor, a board member, or, importantly, someone outside the sector can understand.

2. Why?

Why is this issue important? *(Avoid dhindora peeting - Beating the drum).* This section is where an emotional connection comes in. Use real stories, statistics, and an urgency of sorts to make the donor feel the weight of the cause.

3. Who?

Who will benefit from this funding? Who are the stakeholders involved? Donors want to know the people behind the work, your leadership, the team, and the communities you serve.

4. Where?

Where will the programme take place? Providing location-specific details helps donors visualise the impact.

5. When?

What is the timeline? When will the funds be utilised, and what milestones will be achieved at different stages? Perhaps talking about how sustainable your project or NGO is. A clear roadmap increases credibility.

Keeping these 5 Ws in mind, some key elements every proposal can have include:

1. A Compelling Introduction: A strong opening that grabs attention.

2. The Need Statement: Why this cause matters.

3. Programme Details: How the project will be executed.

4. Impact Metrics: What success looks like.

5. The Budget: Clear, detailed, and justified numbers.

6. Essential Supporting Documents: Legal registrations and certifications.

Striking the Right Balance: How Long Should a Proposal Be?

A good proposal should be long enough to provide clarity and detail but concise enough to keep the donor engaged. The ideal length depends on the donor and the complexity of the project. Here's a quick cheat sheet I wish someone had given me earlier.

1. Small Grant Proposals (2-4 pages): For individual donors, small foundations, or quick funding requests.

2. Corporate or CSR Proposals (5-8 pages): When pitching to companies or CSR divisions, focus on impact, alignment with their CSR goals, and financial clarity.

3. Large Institutional or Government Grants (10-20+ pages): Requires detailed project breakdowns, monitoring frameworks, and extensive financials.

A good rule of thumb:

- Executive Summary: 1 page
- Problem Statement & Need: 1-2 pages
- Programme Details & Methodology: 2-4 pages
- Impact & Measurement: 1-2 pages
- Budgets and Signage: 1-2 pages

The Hidden Secret *(in most cases):* The Budget

I still remember the first time I submitted a proposal that I was sure was perfect. It had everything: our NGO's vision, mission, inspiring impact stories, beautiful images, heartfelt testimonials, and a well-structured budget. I was confident the donor would be moved by our work and approve the funding without hesitation. But when a senior head reviewed the document, they simply flipped through the pages and said, "Let's go straight to the budget."

That was my first big lesson: No matter how compelling your narrative is, the budget is what makes or breaks the deal. Well, *almost.*

Most fundraisers spend 80% of their time perfecting the narrative and only 20% on the budget. But in reality, there are many donors who flip straight to the numbers. This is because organisations making funding decisions, be it their CSR committees, family offices, and corporate boards, want to see financials first. Well, in most cases.

They want to know:

- How much are you asking for?

- How will every rupee be spent?

- Are administrative costs reasonable?

- How much is allocated to direct impact?

- Does your budget reflect a sustainable, well-planned initiative?

The budget is not just a number; it is a story in itself. A well-structured budget with the right line items and sub-line items gives the donor clarity of the spread and opens the door to giving exposure that:

- You are transparent.

- You have thought through every detail.

- You respect their investment.

- You are accountable.

If the budget does not make sense, no matter how heartwarming your proposal is, it might not get past the first screening. So, make sure it's top-notch and well-detailed.

Finance Department: A Friend in Waiting

Talking of the budget, how can we ignore the finance team in the organisation?

Ok, now let's be honest, no department is *truly* your best friend, and finance? Well, they're like that one relative at family gatherings who listens carefully but never quite tells you what's on their mind. You take a step right; finance veers left. It's a peculiar dance, and to this day, I find it amusing. But let's not be too harsh; they don't need judgement; they just need a little reassurance (and maybe a virtual hug) to know you come in peace.

The key here is transparency. Share what you can and encourage them to do the same, at their own pace. And if they prefer moments of isolation to commune with their spreadsheets, respect that too. Over the years, I've always made an effort to befriend finance teams, and sometimes, I've even built genuine connections. But one thing remains certain: they will tell you only what you *need* to know or occasionally, even less.

So, don't take it personally. Work with what you have, earn their trust, and position yourself as the reliable bridge between donors and financial integrity. And if they occasionally vanish into the mysterious realm of audit trails and balance sheets, just smile, nod and let them have their zen. That's their form of yoga.

Presentation Matters: Look the Part

Your proposal should not just read well; it should look professional. High-quality, high-resolution images, sleek formatting, and a well-organised structure can make it look the part. If your proposal looks like a rushed Word document from the early 2000s, donors might assume your work is equally haphazard. The right talent in drafting, editing, and designing is essential. If you don't have it, step up your game and find a way to make it happen. Now with AI, it's definitely possible. Oh, AI! It's like that new relative who just showed up one day, knows everything, gives advice, and now everyone is asking it everything from personal questions to potato recipes!

The first thing I did when I started the job was draft a proposal. Yeah, it's the non-AI era! It was far from perfect. But over time, I learned that a polished, visually appealing proposal can elevate an NGO's credibility and significantly increase its chances of securing funding.

Always Be Prepared: Keep Templates Ready

One thing you will quickly learn as a fundraiser is that donors can be unpredictable. One moment, things seem quiet, and the next, you receive an urgent request: "Can you send us a proposal by EOD?" If you don't have a template ready, you will either scramble to put something together in record time or, worse, miss the opportunity altogether.

Having pre-prepared templates for different types of proposals for small grants, CSR funding, or individual donors can be a lifesaver. Keep them structured, polished, and easily adaptable so that when the time comes, all you need to do is fine-tune the details. Here, in any industry, for that matter, being prepared isn't just helpful but essential, my dear reader.

Let's just say Fundraising without templates is like making Maggi without hot water. It's definitely possible, but unnecessarily painful!

The Power of One Picture

In my earlier banking days in Dubai, life revolved around numbers and processes. My mind was constantly preoccupied with discrepancies, on how to resolve them, and the endless stream of operational challenges that defined my workday. Office politics existed, of course, but being young and naive (which, to be honest, I still am), I never viewed it as a threat. I took life as it came, one day at a time, unburdened by the unseen currents that swirled around me. What really mattered were the Fridays, those precious weekends when my buddies, Sanker and the gang, could escape the monotony. We'd either catch the latest movie, stroll through the sprawling malls, or splurge on some ridiculously overpriced, exclusive dinners that felt like tiny luxuries in our otherwise routine lives.

One weekend, however, was different. I didn't go out. Plans changed, and instead of being out with Sanker, I found myself at home having dinner with my mom and dad. It was an ordinary meal - *pathani roti* and some *alu ka bharta* (mashed potatoes). The kind of simple comfort food that brought warmth to the table. After I finished, my parents still lingered on, chatting softly with their meal while I drifted toward the living room. I settled onto the sofa, my mind still buzzing faintly with work thoughts. That's when my eyes fell on a newspaper lying casually on the coffee table beside me.

Yes, those were the days, the dinosaur era when newspapers were still a thing, crisp and heavy in your hands. I picked it up without much thought, flipping it open somewhere near the middle.

What I saw next hit me with a force I wasn't prepared for.

It was an advertisement. But not the usual kind. This was a two-page spread across the entire section of the newspaper devoted to a single image. There, staring back at me, was a boy. An African boy, maybe six or seven years old. His frame was painfully thin, his bones sharp beneath his skin. His eyes, my God, his eyes were sunken, hollow, yet somehow pleading. Whether from hunger or the harsh reality of famine in his country, his gaze held a weight too heavy for any child to bear. There were no words crowding the page, no overdone pleas for help. Just that image. In the bottom corner, the logo of an international agency rested in small, discreet letters.

The world around me faded. The distant clink of dishes, the low murmur of my parents' conversation, it all blurred into nothingness. My heart clenched as I stared at the picture, trying to process the unfathomable suffering reflected in that child's eyes. Something inside me cracked open.

Without realising it, I folded the paper gently, as if the boy's fragile existence could somehow be disturbed by my carelessness. My legs felt heavy as I stood and walked slowly back to the dining table. My parents were still finishing their meal, tearing soft pieces of roti and dipping them into the gravy, utterly unaware of the storm unravelling inside me.

And then it happened. The dam broke.

I burst into tears. Loud, heaving sobs tore through me as I held down the newspaper. I choked out the words - *Why? Why did this happen to him? Why did that little boy have to suffer? Why couldn't he get help? I also can't do anything for him*. My crying became profuse. My parents froze, stunned by my sudden outpouring. They didn't know how to console me; what words could possibly soften the ache in my chest? So, they let me cry. And I did. I cried as if my tears could somehow bridge the distance between that boy's pain and my helplessness.

For ten long minutes, sorrow wracked my body. When the tears finally slowed, I was drained, empty, as if something vital had been poured out of me. I said nothing more that night. I went to bed in silence while the image of that boy burned into my memory. Sleep came, eventually, but it was restless, haunted by eyes I couldn't unsee.

The next day, I called in and took a leave of absence. I couldn't face the clients, the spreadsheets, the petty office politics, not when my soul felt bruised. I needed time. Time to understand the depth of what I had felt. Time to breathe through the weight of it. And eventually, as time always does, it healed me. Life resumed its usual rhythm. The intensity of that night softened into memory. But something within me had changed forever. And the weekends came back with Sanker and the gang.

That was the moment I realised the power of one picture.

Years later, when I entered the world of fundraising, that image remained with me. I learned a vital lesson from it: when you prepare a proposal, always include a picture. **Not to sell guilt**. Never to manipulate. But to offer a glimpse into the cause. A picture can do what a thousand words cannot; it can speak directly to the heart.

But here's the nuance. You must be careful. Never exploit suffering. Never reduce a human story to a marketing tool. The goal is not to shock someone into giving, nor to burden them with a guilt they cannot carry. Instead, let the image convey the possibility and the difference their generosity can make. Show the need, yes, but also the hope. An image should open doors, not close them.

I would never wish for anyone to feel the crushing sorrow I felt that night. But if a picture can stir someone enough to act, to give, to care, to change a life, then it's worth including. Because sometimes, all it takes is one picture to move the human heart. And when the heart moves, the world moves with it.

Truth Bytes

Bapu, the OG Fundraiser

When we talk about fundraising and resource mobilisation, how can we not mention the real deal, the showstopper, the master of it all, Mahatma Gandhi! The man who could rally millions with nothing but a walking stick and an unshakeable belief. The ultimate influencer before social media, the strategist who turned everyday acts into powerful statements, and the fundraiser who made people give not just their money, but their time and faith. If there was ever a legend in mobilising resources for a cause, it was him. And in the world of fundraising, his lessons still hold true.

Oh yeah, better believe that. *Munna* and *Circuit* will vouch for that too.

Gandhi knew that people don't give because of facts and figures alone. They give because they feel something. He didn't just say, "The British tax on salt is unfair." Instead, he turned it into a gripping narrative: an old man, dressed in white, walking barefoot for miles under the harsh sun, picking up a handful of salt in an act of quiet defiance.

Some fundraisers say 50 million children are out of school. Or they tell stories about one child, Meena, who walks 10 km to school; or Arif, who studies under a streetlamp at night.

You see, facts inform you, but stories inspire action. And sometimes, a little drama always helps.

Building a Movement

Gandhi didn't just raise funds, right? He built movements. His success always lay in making everyone feel like a solid stakeholder in the cause. The rich donated money, but the poor gave their time, and both gave their trust. That's a lesson for every fundraiser where you don't just keep chasing big-ticket donors; you cultivate communities that care. When people feel ownership, they give not just once, but over and over again.

In the end, whether you're a freedom fighter or a fundraiser, the real victory is in getting people to believe. Gandhi proved that a handful of salt could shake an empire. A fundraiser proves that a handful of small donations can change a life.

So, the next time someone asks, "What do fundraisers really do?", you can smile and say, "We march. We mobilise. We make things happen."

I have a tradition to go on social media on 2nd October every year and tell Bapu,

"Happy Birthday Bapu, where's my treat?!"

Chapter 5

Chasing Yes

———— ·●· ————

If you think fundraising is just about asking for money, think again. It's a rollercoaster ride of high-stakes pitches, bizarre encounters, crushing rejections, and victories that appear out of nowhere just when you're about to give up. It's a world where logic often takes a backseat and the most unexpected moments shape your journey.

In the episodes that follow, I pull back the curtain on what truly happens behind the scenes. Perhaps this chapter is the beating heart of the book, the raw, unfiltered reality of fundraising. From cold calls that lead to nowhere or somewhere unexpected to deals that slip away, only to return in the most delightful fashion. From moments that shake your faith to those that restore it in ways you never imagined.

So, fasten your seatbelt. This isn't just a job; it's a test of persistence, luck, and the uncanny power of human connection. And trust me, you won't see what's coming next.

Episode One: The 60-Second Debacle

Fundraising, my friend, is not for the faint-hearted. If you think you've had your share of heartbreaks, try convincing a corporate honcho to part with their CSR funds. There are more "No" responses here than in a high school romance. But hey, as Rocky Balboa once said, "It ain't about how hard you hit. It's about how hard you can get hit and keep moving forward." So, with that spirit, let's dive into one of my early fundraising nightmares. Uh, I mean, experiences.

After dialling an endless stream of wrong numbers, enduring disconnected calls, and speaking to every available receptionist, HR person, and office assistant in sight, I finally made it *(drumroll, please)* to the CSR department head! Yes, I got *the* guy on the call. This was the moment! The golden ticket! My personal FIFA World Cup trophy was within reach.

Now, I am on the phone with him. But before I could break into my victory dance, I could almost feel his exasperation through the phone. The kind of heavy, reluctant sigh that screamed, *Why am I even taking this call?*

Still, I had a job to do. I introduced myself with enthusiasm, trying to mask the anxiety bubbling beneath.

"Which NGO?" he cut in, uninterested.

I barely got through another sentence before he delivered the ultimate reality check: *"Listen, you've got 60 seconds. Tell me what you want."*

Excuse me? Did I just stumble into *The X Factor?* Was I suddenly in a high-stakes speed-pitch competition?

My brain went into overdrive, my tongue into overspeed. What followed was an absolute disaster.

I panicked. Words tumbled out faster than an auctioneer on steroids. I stammered, fumbled, and rambled like my life depended on it. If Eminem had been on the same conference call, he would have tipped his hoodie and said, "Nice try, homie".

And just like that, my 60 seconds were up.

"Try next year. We're not aligned," he declared. *Hangs up.*

I was still holding the phone, talking to nobody. The digital void hummed back at me. Crushed? Absolutely. But did I let it show? Of course not! I took a deep breath and, for the sake of my own dignity, whispered to the ghost on the call, "Thank you, Sir. Next year, please keep us at the top of your priority list."

And then I hung up.

Sigh.

No worries, Wasif. At least I got the call. Later that day, I could tell my CEO a brag story. I proudly announced, "Sir, I spoke to the head of this CSR company today!"

Hey, in fundraising, at times you need to count some losses as wins!

Episode Two: A Tale of Sweat, Silence, and a Pressure Cooker

Ah, LinkedIn. The land of endless connection requests, ignored messages, and the occasional "Happy Work Anniversary" notification from people I don't even remember. This is the story of how I spent more than a year. Yes, a whole year! Trying to get a response from a CSR executive. I sent messages, follow-ups, polite nudges, borderline desperate pleas (okay, not really, but close), and finally, when I had almost made peace with my fate, a miracle happened.

One fine day, my inbox lit up. It wasn't a job scam or an insurance pitch. It was a real response from an actual human being! And not just any human, but an executive from a global pharma giant with operations in India.

Not only did they reply, but they also invited me to an annual CSR conference (online - it's COVID season). A *big deal* where their employees, the top India team, and even the *global* heads would be present. This was massive. And the theme of this event? Their NGO partners! The ones they had supported the previous year and the ones they *might* support this year. This was my shot, my *big* shot.

Now, here's where things got *real*. They gave me two slots:

1. A short and snappy elevator pitch, kind of like 'sell your product in under two minutes'.

2. A detailed proposal presentation, followed by Q&A, aka *the gladiator round*.

Nerve-wracking? Absolutely. But was I excited? Oh, you bet. After all, I had hustled hard for this!

Now, picture this: It was peak COVID. I was working from home, at my parents' place. My wife and kid were staying at her parents' house a few miles away. The house was *my* battleground.

I made one thing very clear to my folks:

"This is huge. I need complete silence. Absolute radio silence. And for the love of everything good in this world, please, no pressure cooker whistles during my call!" My poor mom nodded in solemn agreement.

There I was. *This was it.*

The moment had arrived. The call began. *Game face on.*

Suited up like James Bond on a budget, hair waxed to a shine that could blind satellites, specs so polished they doubled as emergency laser beams. I was ready. The video screens flickered to life one by one. Their global heads all cool, composed, radiating corporate confidence. The India heads visibly stressed, like their souls had just been through a tax audit. (Okay, maybe not that stressed, but you get the picture. And hey, this isn't a dig, it's just vibes.)

Employees and their NGO partners logged in from all over - Mumbai, Chennai, Hyderabad, Gujarat, and Kashmir - each tiny window on my screen a reminder of the *battlefield* I had stepped into.

The host gave an overview of the occasion. The leads came in, dropping gratitude bombs about the previous year's achievements. And then, finally, it was time.

NGOs lined up for their turn, one after the other. I was in the queue, somewhere towards the end. NGOs from Kashmir to Chennai, from Gujarat to Hyderabad, and finally *Mumbai.* My name was called.

Two minutes. Just two minutes.

I delivered my elevator pitch. Was it good? Was it fast? Did I leave them intrigued? *I couldn't tell.* But I felt it. I had given them just enough to want more.

Then a 30-minute break.

I didn't move from my seat. The stakes were *way* too high. My palms were sweaty, but hey, it's Mumbai heat. Manageable. Every passing minute, I whispered to myself, *You got this, man. Jo Jeeta Wohi Sikandar!* (Classic Bollywood flick)

And *then* Round Two.

Screens flickered back to life; fresh faces appeared. Scarier faces. Perhaps the board had walked in. *Stay calm, Wasif. Stay calm,* I told myself.

The host came on. *"And now, we begin the detailed proposal pitches by the NGOs to be selected for the next financial year."*

My heart pounded. *Here it is. No turning back.*

NGOs presented their causes one by one. Then, my moment arrived.

"Aaaand now we have… uhh… Mr… Wasif… Hani!"

Wait. What?

I was caught off guard. My name had just echoed through the speakers like a wrestler making a grand entrance. But no time to react. The host shared my presentation on screen, and I dove in.

For the next 15 minutes, I went on a full-blown rant - facts, figures, passion, fire! In the 16th minute, I finally paused. *"Any questions? Happy to take them here."*

Silence.

20 seconds of pure, terrifying silence.

The host then asked, *"Any questions?"*.

And then an employee from Chennai came through. After a minute of dramatic suspense, he hit me with some *tough* ones.

I answered, stumbling through with a few too many "umms," "I think," and "it's like" fillers. Not the crispest pitch, but hey, I was in the ring, throwing back punches.

And then came the moment. The one that would haunt me for years to come.

From the other room, my mom yells:

"Lunch is around the corner! Can I start the pressure cooker?"

Panic.

I slammed my mic off, covered my laptop camera with my thumb, and yelled back, "Not at all, PLEASE!"

By the time I returned, questions were rolling in one after the other. I powered through until my time was up.

The host thanked me. I had done it. I was thrilled. Excited. I wanted to jump out of my seat.

And the second they moved to the next speaker, I actually did.

I sprinted to my bedroom, yelling "IT'S DONE! I DID IT!" like a child who just nailed his math exam.

And in true *Indian mother's* style, my mom replied:

"Jeete raho beta, jeete raho."(Long life to you, my son.) And I am starting the pressure cooker now!"

Proud, I marched back to my seat, only to see the frozen face of the host staring at me.

Oh.

I looked closer.

This time I *was not on mute.*

Fantastic.

The host, trying to be professional, simply said, *"Thank you, Wasif."* If selected, we will call you."

I gave her a plastic smile and nodded. *"Thank you, yes."* Let's pretend that this didn't happen.

And then, *click.*

She logged me off.

Days passed. Then weeks. Then months.

No call.

We didn't get selected.

Yeah, it hurt. Kind of like a heartbreak.

But hey, I walked away with one hell of a story. And now, I've got to share it with you.

Moral of the story?

You can be the most prepared person in the room. You can suit up, wax your hair, polish your specs, heck, you can even deliver the pitch of your life. Sometimes it's just not the right time. So, we shall wait.

And yeah... you can never, ever control an Indian mother's pursuit of her pressure cooker. So let it be!

Episode Three: The Five-Year Chase

In fundraising and donor relationships, I had learned, it was a game of patience. But nothing could have prepared me for the five-year rollercoaster ride with one particular CSR Head. Let's call him Mr. Elusive.

Year 1: The Introduction

Our first conversation was unexpectedly delightful. Mr. Elusive turned out to be warm, engaging, and passionate about his company's CSR initiatives. We spoke about everything: his work, his past projects, his love for cricket, and even a mutual dislike for Delhi Airport's food court! He had an easy-going charm that made me feel like we had known each other for years. A deep voice, something that you would love to hear on the radio for a long time. I had waited for a while, building the rapport, letting the conversation flow until I finally broke the ice and pitched my NGO's cause, daring to ask the golden question: *Can you be my donor?*

His response? *"Sounds great, but the timing isn't right."* A polite rejection wrapped in possibility. I stepped away, unsure if I would ever hear from him again.

Year 2: A Step Forward

A year later, I felt like trying again, so I reached out fueled by optimism and sent across a carefully crafted email, followed by a phone call. To my surprise, he responded. This time, he seemed more receptive than before.

He asked for a proposal!

I meticulously put together a strong case, highlighting impact numbers, success stories, and carefully aligning our project with his company's CSR goals. I hit 'send' with a hopeful heart and waited. And waited. And waited some more. I couriered an organisation journey booklet to his office. And continued waiting.

Nothing.

Ghosted.

I followed up twice thereafter. His responses became sparse, vague, and non-committal. Something felt off. Had I misread our connection? Had I done something wrong?

I told myself I had to move on, but deep down, I wasn't ready to give up.

Year 3: Conversation Without a Cause

A funny thing happened in the third year when we started talking on the phone again, rare but precious. This time not about work. He'd call out of the blue to chat about life, parents, and the great places Delhi would offer to eat during Ramadan.

At one point, I even joked, *"You do know I'm a fundraiser, right?"* He laughed and said, *"Of course, kaam tho chalthay rahega (work will continue)"*.

It was odd, yet somehow, I played along. Maybe, just maybe, this was all part of that 'game' which these Hollywood heist movies spoke of or the supposedly great conversationalists bragged about – the game?!

Bah!

Maybe trust-building looked different in my world compared to others. Maybe one day, he'd wake up and think, *Hey, let's fund this cheeky guy's NGO.*

That day didn't come... yet.

Year 4: Hope & Heartbreak

By the fourth year, I had lost count of how many times I had followed up. But I was a fundraiser, and if fundraising had a golden rule, it was this: *never take silence as a final answer.*

So, I tried again. This time, to my delight, we finally spoke about work seriously. We discussed specifics, possible funding amounts, and even timelines. My heart raced. This was it? It was happening?!

Until it wasn't.

Something to do with budget cuts, internal shifts, or a misalignment – who knows? Just derailed the process.

I told myself I'd definitely had my heart broken before, but this feeling was different.

Year 5: The Final Push

This was it. This *had* to be it. I had spent four years nurturing this relationship, and I wasn't going to let it fizzle out again.

So, I tried one last time. But this time as a casual heads-up. Nothing focused and definitely not going for war on it. Just happened to throw the dice.

This time, Mr. Elusive didn't just listen, but he actually acted. He asked for a proposal! I submitted one right away, and within weeks, it was approved. The budget was allocated. And just like that, five years of persistence and clear intention paid off. The funding came through.

The feeling was surreal. Five years of calls, emails, meetings, almosts, and near-misses all led to this moment.

If fundraising had taught me anything, it was that some 'Yeses' take time. In this case, it took five years. But when they finally happen, they are *oh so worth it*.

Year 6: Renewal and the Circle of Fundraising

Just when I thought the journey had ended, his now familiar number flashed on my phone a year later. It was him, our very own, Mr. Elusive.

"Hey," he said casually, "we need to discuss something important."

It turns out that the project had gone so well that his company was considering renewing its support. He wanted to explore how they could deepen their impact.

This time, the conversation was different. No ghosting, no endless waiting, just mutual enthusiasm to keep the partnership going. We worked together to refine a fresh proposal, aligned it with their evolving CSR strategy, and before I knew it, another approval came through.

This was a true full-circle moment.

Sometimes you need that foot in the door and sometimes it gets opened by the right person inside the room to respectfully let you in.

Episode Four: The One That Got Away (and Came Back!)

Most fundraisers actively seek out opportunities, reaching out to every possible lead. But this time, I didn't have to chase one down. The opportunity arrived right at my desk.

It started with an unexpected email. A CSR professional had reached out, and not just any CSR professional; this gentleman was from a Dubai-based company. A Dubai connection! My old home! My heart did a little flip. For a moment, I felt like the universe had tossed me a warm hug from across the Arabian Sea. What a beautiful small-world moment!

I wasted no time. We got on a call, and I rolled out my pitch like a magician unveiling his best trick. I spoke about our mission, the impact we had created, and the big dreams we had for the future. It felt like catching up with an old friend, one who understood where I came from and why this work mattered.

And guess what? It worked. Well, almost. He put our NGO on the shortlist for funding. We were now in the running with seven or eight other NGOs, all vying for the final selection.

The rounds began. First, a verbal pitch. Nailed it. Then, a proposal submission. Done. Then an application form, filled out like a pro. Due diligence came in, every legal document combed through and every financial statement scrutinised. It was like playing an intense game of chess, one careful move at a time. Finally, it was out of my hands. My Dubai guy would now present our case to his CSR committee.

A week later, my phone rang. I braced myself.

"Hey, Wasif! Congrats!"

Oh yeah, Habibi! It had to happen. I mean, come on! *Ghar ka mamla tha!* (It was a home affair!)

My eyebrows shot up. "So, how much of the budget was approved?"

There was a pause. "Well... you have made it to the final round now. It's down to you and one more NGO. The committee decides today."

My excitement deflated like a sad balloon. "One more round? Damn."

But I played it cool. No over-excitement, no over-confidence. Just a silent prayer to the CSR gods. I imagined a dramatic scene playing out in their boardroom. A battle of presentations, impact reports flying across the table, arguments made in favour of my NGO. And then, the final decision. *(Honestly, this scene doesn't play out in reality, mind you, I was imagining)*

That evening, as promised, the call came.

"Hi Wasif, the other NGO has been chosen."

Silence.

I was crushed. *Dubai ki company hai, yaar!* (It's a Dubai company, man!) How could this happen? This was supposed to be a homecoming victory! I felt like a cricketer who had reached 99 runs and then got out. So close, yet so far.

But I swallowed my disappointment and put on my best 'gracious loser' voice. "No worries, let's try again next year."

His response was warm. "For sure."

I hung up, satisfied that I had given it my best shot. But I knew one thing: this wouldn't make it to my year-end KPIs. It was a lost cause... or so I thought.

Fast forward exactly one year

My phone rang, and I saw his name flash on the screen. This time, I answered as if we were childhood buddies who had spent countless nights eating shawarma and sipping black tea on Al Rigga Street in Deira.

"How's it going, man?" I bellowed, my excitement unfiltered.

He laughed. "Hey Wasif, nice to hear you. Do you guys need laptops?"

I said, "Yeah, sure, we do! What's the deal?"

He explained that their CSR programme was procuring brand-new laptops for beneficiaries. Would it fit our cause? I mean... was that even a question?!

Within record time, I drafted the proposal, tweaked last year's documents and submitted everything. This time, it felt different. It felt like destiny.

A few days later, his call came again.

"The committee has given the go-ahead."

And then, the words that sealed the deal:

"We've chosen your NGO."

I nearly danced in my office. **Wallah, humko Dubai ka CSR pasand kartee!** (Swear by God, Dubai CSR loves me!)

We received the laptops, and our beneficiaries under the education programme thrived because of it. It was more than just funding; it was validation, proof that some things are just meant to be. So, give it time and if it has to come, it will come.

And as for my new Dubai *wala* friend? Well, he still calls every year, offering furniture, oxygen cylinders, or whatever else their CSR budget allows. And every time, I chuckle and say, "Thanks, but that doesn't fit my programme."

The lesson I learned a little differently here was that not every lost deal is truly lost. Some just take a scenic route back to you. Keep the faith, keep the connections, and sometimes, CSR comes knocking when you least expect it.

Episode Five: The Ghosted Emails

Some doors you knock on once, and they open. Others take a battering ram of tenacity before they even creak. And then there are those doors you knock on so many times, you eventually give up, only to have them swing open when you least expect it.

This is one of those stories.

It started with a global company, one of those towering giants with its footprint in every corner of the world. The kind of company you dream about getting funding from.

I had a lead for reaching them. And in fundraising, leads are gold. They have hidden power like buried treasure waiting to be discovered.

This particular lead came from our own CEO, who mentioned a contact from the company to me. Armed with nothing but an email address and a deck, I crafted my first email. A soft pitch, nothing too pushy. Just an introduction, a brief on our work, and an attachment filled with some impact numbers and smiling beneficiaries.

The First Email

Here it begins. I stared at the blinking cursor before hitting send. You know that moment; it's like the final hesitation before you put yourself out there. A deep breath, a hopeful thought, and then... click. The email was sent.

It was professional yet warm. I introduced myself, briefly outlined our work, and attached a neatly designed deck packed with powerful impact statistics. Nothing overwhelming, just a snapshot of how their company could make a difference.

I imagined the recipient opening the email, intrigued by the subject line, scrolling through the deck, feeling a tug of interest. Maybe they'd forward it to a colleague. Maybe they'd even hit "Reply" with a "Let's discuss."

But reality had other plans.

Hours passed. Then days. I refreshed my inbox a little too often. I did not get any response. Maybe they were busy? Maybe my email got buried under a pile of corporate to-dos? Maybe - just maybe - there was a technical glitch, and it never even reached them?

I held onto hope. But the silence was deafening.

No response. Nothing. Not even an automated out-of-office reply to give me false hope. It's fine. Let's just tone it down but not stop.

The Second Email

Fine. I sent a second email. This time, I adjusted the tone, made it a little more engaging. Maybe the first one had been too formal? Still, no response. Not even a polite "Thank you for reaching out, but we're not interested."

The Third Email

Alright, third time's the charm. You see, the third email is always the tricky one. It carries the weight of hope. You convince yourself that this is the one. This is the email that will finally get a reply, even if it's just a half-hearted "Apologies for the delay" or a fake "Sorry, I missed this earlier."

But the world doesn't work that way. No response. Again.

The Quarterly Reminders

By now, I should have let it go. But instead, I decided to turn this into a long-term experiment. Once a quarter, like clockwork, I sent a follow-up email. Not too aggressive, just a gentle nudge. A "Hey, in case you missed this…" kind of thing. And every quarter, I got the same response - absolute nothingness.

The Decision to Move On

A year passed. And that was it. I was done. I wasn't going to chase a ghost anymore. Some doors just don't open, and I had better things to do. So, I closed the file in my mind and moved on.

The Unexpected Call

Until six months later, when my phone rang.

The number was unfamiliar; I am thinking, is this going to be that "Do you need a loan or overdraft facility" phone call? I said to myself, c'mon man, let's pick up. Let's politely tell the banker I don't need it and wish the person all the very best. Being an ex-banker, I kind of have a soft corner for their sales pursuit. Can imagine their pressure.

I pick up the call.

An energetic person from the other side starts speaking, "Hi there! I recently stepped into this role and came across your emails in my predecessor's inbox. Your emails caught my attention, and I couldn't help but be curious. I have to ask, what exactly does your NGO do?"

Oh boy. Here we *goooooooo!*

The Outcome

What followed was a series of conversations, each one more promising than the last. She wasn't just being polite; she was genuinely interested. And eventually, those ghosted emails turned into something real. Not in the way I had originally imagined, there was no big fat cheque at the end of it. But instead, we received in-kind donations that made a tangible difference to our beneficiaries and staff. And honestly, that felt like a win.

So, what's the lesson here?

Tenacity pays off, but not always in the way you expect. Sometimes, the seeds you plant take longer to sprout. Sometimes, they don't grow at all. But every once in a while, they bloom when you least expect it.

And that's why, in fundraising and in life, you keep knocking. You never know which door will eventually open.

Episode Six: The Unfinished Goodbye

It was a regular morning when my phone buzzed with an unknown number. I hesitated for a moment before answering, but curiosity got the better of me. A lady on the other end spoke in a crisp, professional tone. She wanted to visit our NGO, mentioning that her organisation was scouting for potential partners and exploring if there was a match in vision and approach. Without a second thought, I invited her to visit.

The next day arrived quicker than expected. I was always the early bird at work, but to my surprise, as I walked through the main gate, I found her arriving just a step ahead of me. The sky was still painted with shades of dawn, and the office hadn't even come to life yet. We exchanged polite nods as I held the gate open for her and escorted her to the meeting room. Entering the room with a swift motion, I pulled out a chair for her, switched on the lights, the fan, and the air conditioner. Being the ever-hospitable Indian, I asked her whether she would fancy a cup of tea or coffee. Her response was as unexpected as her early arrival.

"Black coffee. No sugar," she said without a hint of hesitation.

I was momentarily taken aback. In my time, most visitors preferred the safe choice of tea or a regular coffee, sweetened to their liking. But her preference was as bold as the aura she carried. I peeked outside the meeting room, hoping the office boy had arrived. Predictably, he had not. I rushed to find someone who could assist, and luckily, my favourite colleague was already at her desk. I explained the situation in a flurry, and without saying a word, she gestured with her index finger for me to follow her to the pantry.

The two of us entered the pantry, staring at the utensils and the drawers. Yup, now transformed into an impromptu culinary team, flinging open drawers and hunting for the essentials. The clock ticked on, but I had one mission: to deliver her black coffee. My dear colleague boiled the water, added the coffee grounds, stirred it slowly, letting the aroma rise like a quiet promise. With the coffee finally brewed, I placed it carefully on a tray, grabbed some tissues for good measure, and made my way back to the meeting room with the finesse of a Michelin-starred waiter.

The conversation that followed was nothing short of exhilarating. She wanted to know everything. The origins of our organisation, the impact we had made, and the vision we held for the future. I took her on a tour of the premises, sharing anecdotes and milestones. When it was time to part ways, I walked her to her cab, and just as she settled in, she turned to me with a phrase that every fundraiser dreams of hearing.

"Send me the proposal. And ask for a larger bucket."

The words echoed in my mind long after her car disappeared into the city's chaos. I raced to my CEO, excitement barely contained, and blurted out the opportunity. He was rushing off to another meeting but waved me on, saying, "Yes, just send it." That was all the permission I needed. I dived into the proposal with unwavering focus, crafting a comprehensive plan, leaving no detail unattended. By the end of the day, it was in her inbox.

Weeks slipped by. I checked in with her regularly, and each time she would reassure me to hold on. Then, the unimaginable happened. The world came to a halt as COVID-19 unleashed its fury. The proposal vanished into the abyss of uncertainty, buried under more pressing global concerns. Worse still, the amazing lady I had been engaging with became redundant as the company restructured. My dreams of securing the deal crumbled.

Yet, something within me refused to let go entirely. I checked on her periodically, sending well-wishes and even sharing job opportunities when they crossed my path. Months stretched into two long years, and our conversations remained sporadic but warm. I thought nothing more would come of it until one evening, after dinner, my phone rang again.

Her voice was lighter, almost playful. "Hey, I got a job," she announced, followed by a soft chuckle.

"Where?" I asked, curiosity piqued.

"Same place," she said. "I'm now Chief of Staff."

A chill ran down my spine. Fate, it seemed, had a sense of irony. With cautious hope, I asked the question lingering at the edge of my thoughts. "Do you have anything in mind? Should I send a proposal?"

She paused, then casually said, "Why not?"

I sprang into action. My CEO barely let me finish the story before giving me the green light. The next morning, the proposal was on her desk. What followed was a tense series of calls and deliberations between her company's board members and my senior executives. From my office window,

I watched the world move while my heart beat in a rhythm of anxious anticipation.

Then, one afternoon, my CEO called me into his office. His face was unreadable. I held my breath. "Wasif, it's approved," he said softly.

The deal was unlike anything I had ever closed. It wasn't just a donation; it was a partnership. They signed a three-year agreement to support us. It felt like the universe was rewarding the loyalty and care I had shown during the uncertain times.

The partnership began. Year one passed smoothly. In year two, an additional expense I pitched was approved without question. It felt like we were unstoppable.

But the winds began to change. In the third year, whispers of restructuring surfaced. I ignored them at first, confident that our relationship was strong. Until one day, a formal letter arrived. The company was winding up. All partnerships would be terminated, including ours.

I sat in my office, numb. It was over. Just like that, our three-year journey ended without a proper goodbye. There were no celebratory final calls, no handshakes, and no farewell meeting. Just an email, cold and final. I kept staring at the letter, hoping to find some hidden clause or fine print that would reverse the decision. But there was nothing. It was done.

I couldn't help but think of the movie *Life of Pi*, where Pi reflects on how the hardest part of letting go is not getting the chance to say goodbye. That thought echoed through my mind, settling deep in the pit of my heart. After everything we had built together, it felt wrong to have it end in silence.

Perhaps it was naive to think that some relationships are immune to the inevitability of endings. I replayed the beginning over and over. Her early arrival, the black coffee, the first proposal, the second proposal and the thrill of that approval. It had felt like destiny. But now, it felt like a dream that was going well until I woke up and saw no end to it.

I often wonder if I should reach out again. Maybe I will. After all, some bonds deserve more than an abrupt ending. For now, I hold on to the belief that when you give something good to the universe, it gives you something back, even if it takes a little longer. And perhaps, somewhere down the road, our paths will cross again, and this time, I will take a moment to say goodbye properly.

Truth Bytes

The Storyteller

Facts inform. But stories, they move hearts.

You can walk into a room with charts, reports, and numbers that gleam with promise. But if a donor doesn't *feel* it, they won't fund it.

Because fundraising isn't just about information. It's about *emotion*. It's about making someone care enough to act.

It's the story of a child whose very first school bag unlocked a future.

A mother who held a book and read her first word with tears in her eyes.

A father who, for the first time, told his son, *"Go ahead. Dream."*

A volunteer whose single act of kindness became the spark for a movement.

These are not anecdotes. These are living, breathing testaments that hope works when we believe in it enough to share it.

As a fundraiser, you are not just collecting money.

You are *offering meaning.*

You are *inviting belief.*

You are saying, *"This matters. And so can you."*

So gather those stories.

Hold them close.

Tell them with honesty, with humility, and with a wide-open heart.

Because when the numbers fade and the data falls flat,

It's the story that stays behind.

And it's the story that moves someone to say "Yes."

Chapter 6

Heartbreaks

They say heartbreak in love is the most exquisite agony, which is soft in its arrival, but savage in its staying. It carves silence into your laughter, turns memories into minefields, and leaves behind a haunting ache where once there was warmth.

But have you ever heard about the heartbreak of a fundraiser? If not, let me take you there.

I was staring at my inbox, reading the words over and over: "We regret to inform you that we won't be moving forward." Three months of calls, emails, due diligence, and endless grant writing were gone. Just like that. And all I could think was: Why does this feel like getting dumped over a text?

Imagine pouring your soul into something. Chasing a dream with relentless passion. Nurturing a relationship that felt almost destined. Building something from scratch, watching it take shape, feeling it grow stronger with every interaction. And then, just when you think you have it, just when it seems within your grasp, it vanishes. Slips through your fingers like sand. Leaves you standing there, stunned, empty-handed, and wondering what just happened. That feeling is brutal. It does not matter how experienced you are. It does not matter how many times you have faced disappointment before. When it happens, it shatters you. You can actually hear the cracks in your chest.

It's the same in love where you get the heartbreak, especially when there is no closure. The person you were madly in love with moved on to someone else. Or the person just stopped talking to you, maybe because you were not interesting enough. Or the person had other priorities, be it greener pastures or someone offering them better security than you. And you are left there, holding nothing but memories and questions that will *never* be answered.

In fundraising, it is the same. The unanswered emails. The enthusiastic calls that turn into silence. The last-minute cancellations that leave you staring at your inbox, refreshing the page, hoping for a reply that will never come. The polite but brutal response. "No, we are not going ahead."

I have lived through these moments more times than I can count. And let me tell you this. You will not die!

It will definitely sting. It will make you want to scream into a pillow or stare at the ceiling for hours, wondering why. But you will survive. So, let's read on.

There were times when I was sure, as in absolutely sure, that a deal was about to be sealed. The proposal was strong. The conversations were warm. The decision-makers were nodding, smiling, engaging. It was all leading up to that magical "Yes." And then, just when the universe seemed to be aligning in my favour, something happened. A budget freeze. A change in leadership. An unexpected competitor swooping in. Saw the bureaucracy play in. And any plot twists that leave you in such a shock that you would play Justin Timberlake's '*Cry Me a River*' all day on loop.

The first time this happened, I felt like my world had collapsed. The emotional weight of rejection is something no one warns you about in fundraising. We talk about resilience, persistence, the art of persuasion - but not the ache of a deal that almost was. Not the gut-punch of an eleventh-hour fallout. Not the sleepless nights spent replaying every conversation, every email, wondering where it went wrong. And the worst part? You never truly get a convincing answer.

Dreaded Silent Phase

There's a worst phase of all, and it's when the market is silent. No calls, no emails, no donor meetings, just you, your inbox, and the sound of your own existential crisis. This is the part where even your spam folder looks tempting because at least someone, somewhere, wants to reach out to you (even if it's that unknown prince from that country you never heard of offering you millions – *the spam mails, duh!*).

You refresh your emails over and over, hoping for a reply that does not come. You glance at your phone, convincing yourself you might have missed a call. You stare at the screen, willing a notification to pop up. Anything. Even a rejection would be better than this empty silence. Yeah, you know that feeling, don't you?

This is where self-motivation becomes your lifeline. The trick is to accept the silence, not as defeat, but as an opportunity. Fill the void with purpose. Pour yourself into something productive, something that reminds you of why you started this in the first place. Because silence does not mean the game is over. Or a 'No, we can't go ahead' doesn't mean it's over. It simply means *the next move is yours.*

Surviving the Fall

Rejection is a punch to the gut. It knocks the wind out of you. Makes you question everything. You tell yourself it's just business, but it feels personal. And that's because it is. You gave it your time, your energy, your belief. Now, it's okay to feel like hell. But staying there? That's not an option.

So how do you handle this? How do you stop yourself from falling into the abyss of despair? Let's take a look at some pointers that will help you climb out of the ditch you've created.

1. **Feel it, but don't drown in it**

   The worst thing you can do is pretend it doesn't hurt. It does. Acknowledge the loss. Let yourself feel the sting of disappointment. But don't let it consume you. Give yourself a timeframe to sulk, scream, or cry if you must. Yeah, and big boys do cry, and there's nothing wrong with that! You pick yourself up. Because dwelling too long in rejection turns it into a prison. Let that monkey off your back.

2. **Detach your worth from the outcome**

   Fundraising, like love, is unpredictable. It's not always about how hard you worked or how perfect your pitch was. Sometimes, external forces derail the best-laid plans. Your worth as a fundraiser isn't defined by one rejection or even ten. Keep reminding yourself of that. A "No" doesn't mean you weren't good enough. It means it wasn't the right fit. Or the right time. Or the right people. Whatever way, better keep in mind it's not your loss.

3. Dissect, but don't obsess

Analyse what went wrong, but don't overanalyse to the point of self-blame. Was there something you could have done differently? Did you miss a red flag? Learn from it, make notes, adjust your approach but don't let the past haunt your future pitches. Overthinking doesn't close deals. Action does.

4. Redirect the energy

When a deal falls apart, the worst thing you can do is let that negativity bleed into your next attempt. Instead, pour your energy into something productive. Dive into research. Strengthen your pitch. Find another potential donor who might just be the right fit. Channel the energy and release it in the right direction.

5. Remember: A *No* isn't always forever

Just like in life, timing is everything. I've had deals that seemed dead come back months or even years later, revived under unexpected circumstances. A "No" today doesn't mean a "No" forever. Stay connected. Stay hopeful. You never know what doors might reopen. Because today's "No" can be tomorrow's "Let's talk".

Rising from the Ashes

Heartbreak, whether in love or in fundraising, can either break you or build you. The greatest lovers and the most legendary fundraisers aren't the ones who never face rejection. They are the ones who learn to take the hit, embrace the pain, and come back stronger.

Rejection will come. That is the brutal truth of this journey. But so will victories, the kind that taste even sweeter because they rise from the ashes of failure. And in those moments, the triumphs that follow your darkest setbacks will feel like redemption.

So, stand tall. Feel the sting but don't let it define you. Rise again and again because the best stories are written by those who refuse to stay down.

Refuse to stay down, player.

Suit up, put on your war paint, and step again into the arena. It is time to become the G!

You know why? Because heartbreaks don't stop, and neither do we.

Truth Bytes

SOPs Don't Kill Magic.
They Make It Repeatable

Charisma can open doors. A powerful story, a spark in your voice, the right words at the right time… these are the visible traits of a great fundraiser. But what happens after the room stops clapping? What happens when the spotlight fades and the curtain falls?

Fundraising may feel spontaneous, a rush of connection, a moment of magic. But the truth is, behind every 'lucky' win lies a rock-solid system. Behind every big donor callback and every last-minute breakthrough is a well-established Standard Operating Procedure (SOP).

The follow-up tracker, the CRM update, the proposal template, the impact deck, knowing what information can be shared and what must remain confidential. These are not mundane details. They are the architecture holding up your brilliance. They are the reason your charisma doesn't just dazzle; it delivers.

A clear, step-by-step procedure does not limit you. It empowers you. It reassures the donor: we are not improvising, we are prepared. We are not chasing luck; we are following a standard. It tells the world that behind the sparkle is a structure. That behind the passion is professionalism.

And when you are no longer alone, that is when you are leading a team; it becomes even more important that every member understands the dos and don'ts from day one.

Clarity cannot wait. It must be the foundation. Everyone should know what to speak, what to share, what to hold back, and how to respond when stakes are high. When this is done right, your team walks into any room with confidence, not confusion. They are not guessing; they are grounded. A process is not a mere suggestion. It is law. It is scripture. It is the quiet force that shapes consistency, trust, and success.

Chapter 7

Becoming the World's Greatest Relationship Manager

What are you really chasing?

Is it the numbers?

The recognition?

The next big donor?

It all boils down to one thing, and that's becoming *The World's Greatest Relationship Manager!*

When I worked with the Arabs, they often shared wisdom in the simplest yet most profound ways. "Ya Wasif, keep this sweet," they would say, pointing to their tongues. At first, I did not fully understand, but over time, the meaning became clear. It was not just about choosing the right words; it was about how those words were delivered. It was about tone, intention, and grace. A conversation, a negotiation, even a follow-up. Everything had to be done in a way that left the other person feeling good. It was a lesson in respect, in patience, and in the quiet power of sincerity.

That's when I realised something profound. The most important organ in shaping a true relationship manager is not the hands that sign contracts, nor the eyes that scan reports but the tongue. The way we speak, connect, and inspire trust sets us apart. And that's where the journey to becoming a legendary relationship manager begins.

The Foundation: Owning the Relationship

Growing up in the banking world, right in the thick of branch banking, I was exposed to different kinds of relationship managers. From mass banking to mid-markets, premier clients to royalty, one thing became crystal clear: The RM is more than just a banker; they are the bridge between the institution and the client. That one handshake confirms the bridge. You better believe it.

There are relationship managers, then good relationship managers, and then there are the great relationship managers.

The first kind follows instructions exactly as given. They do what is expected, adhere to the rules, and meet targets just enough to stay in the game. They complain about the system, feel frustrated with their workload, and are disappointed when the bonus does not meet expectations. But they do their job, nothing more and nothing less.

Then there is the good relationship manager. Someone who understands that service is not just about transactions but about building connections. They go beyond the script, adding warmth and attentiveness. They listen, anticipate needs, and offer solutions that make clients feel valued.

They do not just chase numbers but focus on meaningful connections. Read carefully – *connections*.

And then there is the great relationship manager, the one who transcends service to create a relationship experience. They don't wait for opportunities; they uncover them. They don't merely meet expectations; they redefine them. For them, relationships aren't items to be ticked off a list; they are a living craft. With every interaction, they transform a casual conversation into a lasting bond and a standard pitch into a moment of genuine trust.

What sets them apart? What makes them extraordinary?

Let's explore more.

A great relationship manager does more than serve clients; they earn their trust in a way that lasts. Clients don't just engage with them; they choose to follow them. Their loyalty isn't anchored to the bank, but to the person who made them feel seen, heard, and truly valued. It is not the brand they return to; it is *you*. And there is no greater validation of your work than hearing a client say, "Excuse me, I only want to talk to Wasif. Please call him." That moment, that sound, that acknowledgement marks the beginning of greatness. That is when you stop being just an employee and become the torchbearer of trust.

The same principle holds true in the non-profit world. Here, we don't manage bank accounts; we manage *faith*. The funds we raise are not just numbers; they represent lives transformed, trees planted, children educated, injustices prevented, and so on.

Your donors definitely need a zillion narrative impact reports along with the financial reports, according to their formats! But there is a stratosphere above these paper requirements, it's *reassurance* that you are there and you shall deliver! They need to know their money is safe, that it is being used with integrity, and that their contribution is more than a transaction. It is a *legacy*.

Fundraising Doesn't Choose You. It Will Eventually Find You

When I completed my postgraduate development course at a premier institute in Mumbai, I applied for all kinds of roles. From impact assessment, monitoring and evaluation, programme management, heck, even HR. Trying to find where I truly belonged. As I thought. Each rejection or near miss left me questioning if I was on the right path.

Then came a conversation with my beloved professor, Mr. Kaustav Majumdar. A moment that has stayed with me ever since. He looked at me and said something I'll never forget: "If I had to give my money to someone for a good cause, I would give it to you."

That moment was an eye-opener. I had come from a world where the sales brass bankers exuded success in every step. They walked into meetings in sharp suits, wrists adorned with Omegas or Rolexes, the latest phones in hand, and the clink-clank of the chunky car keys casually jingling. A subtle but deliberate reminder that luxury was a given. It was a culture where status spoke before words did, where a Montblanc wallet was placed on the table first, with an iPhone resting neatly on top, as if setting the stage before the conversation even began.

The industry glorified polished exteriors and power dressing. And oh yeah, how can we forget the cars! The top model cars. But here was my beloved professor, whom I affectionately now call *Kaustav Da*, reminding me that the essence of fundraising is *trust*. It is not about the loudest voice in the room or the sleekest pitch deck. Or even becoming India's next top model. It is about the honesty you bring to the table. The quiet confidence that makes a donor *believe in you*.

That one sentence shifted everything. It made me realise that fundraising wasn't just about numbers. It wasn't just another 'sales job'. It was about trust, relationships, and belief. Becoming the right...*wait up*...let's just say the righteous salesman or, if I may say, the righteous relationship manager of funds.

That night, I stopped second-guessing and applied for my first vacancy in fundraising. And just like that, I got it. All this time, I had been searching for the right role, but in the end, the right role found me.

Kaustav Da and I still keep in touch from time to time throughout the year. I hope he enjoyed the little Batmobile Hot Wheels I once gifted him. A small token for someone who continues to hold a big place in my journey. Just a quiet thank you to him, through these pages, for always being so generous with his knowledge and spirit.

The Art of Fundraising

Most people think fundraising is just about asking for money. But the best fundraisers know it is never about the ask. It is about building relationships so strong that donors *want* to give.

I learned this the hard way.

My early days fundraising pitches had all the right ingredients, or so I thought. I had my numbers, my stories, and my polished deck ready to impress. I walked into the call with confidence, delivered my pitch with enthusiasm, and watched as the donor listened, nodded, and said, "Sounds great, send me an email."

I sent the email. No reply. I followed up. Still nothing.

A month later, I ran into the same donor at an event. He smiled, greeted me warmly, and even said he remembered our conversation. Later, I realised he had made the generous donation to someone else.

That moment changed everything. I realised that fundraising is not about presenting a perfect case; it is about making a real connection. A pitch might spark interest, but only trust leads to commitment. And this trust-building exercise will take time. So don't lose patience.

A strong pitch can open the door, but exceptional service is what keeps it open. Numbers and presentations will only take you so far. What truly matters is trust, follow-through, and consistency. Without that, the donor is not choosing *you*. They are choosing the brand you represent. And if that is the case, you will end up just as another facilitator of a transaction, easily replaceable and quickly forgotten.

Building real relationships takes time. But that is what transforms a one-time gift into a lasting partnership.

They understand the system like the back of their hand, and within its framework, they craft a path that is unmistakably their own, original, bold, and deeply authentic. Yet never once do they compromise the core values that hold it all together. Now that is greatness. Don't aim to be just another rockstar trying to break the rules. Be the phenomenon who masters them and becomes the example others rise to emulate. Because true influence is not about disruption for the sake of noise, but about direction that sparks transformation.

The Gentle Power of Follow-Ups

Great relationship managers excel at something far more valuable than just making a sale or securing a deal. They master the art of staying relevant without being intrusive, of 'following up' without feeling like they are chasing. They know that true success is not about how many times you reach out, but *how* you do it.

Following up is an art that requires balance, intuition, and finesse. When done poorly, it feels like an annoyance, an unwelcome intrusion that pushes people away. But when done right, it becomes an act of nurturing, a subtle yet powerful way to keep the conversation alive and build genuine connections.

A good follow-up is never a demand. It is a thoughtful reminder, a gentle nudge that keeps you relevant without being overbearing. It is not about pressuring someone into a response but about reinforcing your presence in a way that adds value rather than creating discomfort.

True professionals understand that timing and tone make all the difference. A well-crafted follow-up builds trust instead of testing patience. It shows consistency, reliability, and a genuine interest in the relationship beyond just the transaction.

When done with grace, a follow-up does more than just secure a reply. It earns respect. It shifts your position from being just another requester to being a trusted partner, someone worth engaging with, remembering, and ultimately choosing to work with.

Please don't be under the impression that sending them a "gentle reminder" email every day will do the trick. They will eventually either block you, file a restraining order, or worst of all drag your screenshots onto LinkedIn with a post that starts with, *"Dear Fundraiser, please stop doing this..."* and ends with 500+ reactions, a trending hashtag, and your boss awkwardly forwarding it to you with, *"Any Thoughts?"*.

Donor Retention: The True Test of a Great RM

If you think securing the donation is the finish line, think again. That is just the warm-up.

The real challenge begins when a client converts to a donor. This is where the true World's Greatest Relationship Manager emerges.

Stewardship is a process. And in it, *patience* is everything. Some donors will ask for endless reports, spreadsheets, and justifications, as if you are running a multinational corporation rather than a social impact programme. Others will come with requests so impossible that even a magician would struggle to pull them off. But saying no is not always an option, because let's be honest, the "higher-ups" would rather see you sweat it out than see a donor walk away.

Then there are the ones who test you, not just your endurance, your diplomacy, but on particularly bad days, your very will to exist.

But here's the secret. A donor who asks a thousand questions is not indifferent; they are *invested*. Their scrutiny is not a burden; it is an opportunity. It also means they have processes by their higher-ups, even if they express it in ways that make you want to meditate, scream, or both.

And you have to be ready for all of them. Some will be warm, engaged, and enthusiastic. Others will transform the moment the ink dries on the cheque. One day, they are charming, full of smiles, and eager to help. The next day, they have turned into an entirely different person, questioning every penny, every decision, and possibly your entire career choice.

Dr. Jekyll one day. Mr. Hyde the next. Be ready for that player. No time for culture shocks.

And through it all, you must remain calm, composed, and smiling because the best relationship managers know that keeping a donor is an art form. And in this fraternity, the real work *always* starts after the handshake.

Beware of those who are not donors yet but will happily lead you on with false hopes, endless requests for documents, and never-ending "internal discussions." Experience will teach you to spot them early. Invest your time wisely. Chasing shadows does not fund your cause.

The Silent Victory of Renewals

There is a rare and quiet satisfaction in securing a donor renewal. Unlike the rush of landing a new donor, this victory doesn't come with grand celebrations or congratulatory pats on the back. It unfolds subtly, sometimes with a single-line confirmation in an email, sometimes in a call that lasts less than a minute.

But beneath that simplicity lies something profound.

A renewal is more than just another year of funding; it is an unspoken acknowledgement that you did something right. It means the donor didn't just see the reports, you made them feel the impact. It means they weren't just politely responding to emails, they trusted the person behind them. It is a vote of confidence, a signal that your work wasn't just compelling in the beginning but remained worthy of support long after the first commitment was made.

This victory isn't won through a single pitch or a perfectly crafted proposal. It is built in the unnoticed moments, the email answered at 10 pm because the donor had a last-minute query, the extra effort taken to ensure a field visit runs smoothly, the unexpected arrival of the client's auditor and your finance team accommodating them without hesitation, the honesty in sharing both successes and setbacks.

It is the product of consistency, patience, and the ability to make a donor feel not like a funder but a partner.

Along the way, there are times when we overlook pressures, let go of frustrations, and navigate moments that may feel unfair or even disheartening. Because in the end, what truly matters is trust.

The Greatest RM does not have a script. They don't panic; they pause, observe, and adapt. And after all the shocks absorbed, when the donor renews the partnership without hesitation, that, my dear reader, is the silent victory.

The Power of Referrals

There's no greater testament to your work than a donor personally vouching for you to another. It's more than just a referral; it's an unspoken seal, a quiet yet powerful validation that your efforts have made an impact. In that moment, it's as if they're taking your hand and placing it in the palm of someone who shares the same vision, someone ready to support you just as fiercely or perhaps even more.

Of course, a referral does not guarantee an easy path. You will still have to navigate the ordeal, from rigorous due diligence to intense scrutiny to the endless paperwork that will follow. There will be interviews, site visits, and repeated questions that make you feel like you are moving in circles. But that introduction transforms what could have been a long and uncertain outreach into a warm and promising opportunity. And when, after all of this, you finally convert the referral on board, the victory feels even sweeter. It is not just about securing the funding, but about knowing that your work spoke for itself before you ever stepped into the room.

And don't forget to call the angel who referred you. Acknowledge them. Appreciate them. Never, ever let that gratitude slip through the cracks; it matters more than you think.

Thank you, Ms. Tabassum Aranjo, for being that angel in my journey.

The Reality of Competition

No matter how often we call them 'colleagues from different institutions', the reality is they are also competitors, each vying for support from the same limited pool of funding that you eye. You pour your heart into a proposal, clear every hurdle, and make it to the final round, only to watch the funding slip away to another organisation. Sometimes it is external politics, sometimes strategic priorities, sometimes a stronger relationship than yours, and sometimes it simply comes down to their personal preference, perhaps a shared vision, or even a gut feeling. No matter what the reasons are, the disappointment will be real.

But in this world, resilience is everything. Instead of dwelling on the loss, keep the door open. A warm follow-up, a sincere thank you, and a gentle reminder to consider you in the next cycle can make all the difference. Because in this field, persistence is what keeps you moving forward. As they say, just keep swimming.

The Power of Owning Mistakes:
Turning Flaws into Trust

There are many moments in every donor relationship when things don't go as planned. A flaw emerges, sometimes an oversight, sometimes an unexpected challenge, or maybe an inability to allocate all of the funds within the agreed time frame. In these moments, the best course of action is to own up to it.

The response can go either way, but taking responsibility is the only way forward.

I remember one such instance when we realised a reporting error in a grant we had received. The funds had been allocated correctly, but the utilisation report contained discrepancies that could create confusion. I decided to call the donor immediately instead of waiting for them to find out and revert to me.

The reaction? A disaster. The donor overreacted, questioning our credibility, and for a moment, it felt like the relationship was crumbling. But instead of getting defensive, we focused on solutions. We reworked the report, provided the required data, demonstrated transparency in how we addressed the issue, and redid our impact calculations. Eventually, we realigned the reporting within agreed terms on time.

On another occasion, a project milestone faced delays due to unforeseen challenges of fund utilisation. Instead of waiting for the donor to follow up, we proactively informed them of the issue. This time, the response was different. The donor understood that we were already working to resolve it. By keeping them in the loop, we gave them confidence that their investment was being prioritised.

In both cases, the flaw remained, but the difference was in how we handled it. Owning the problem and keeping the donor informed is where you are working on a potential crisis into an opportunity to reinforce trust. Because, at the end of the day, accountability isn't just about fixing mistakes; it's about ensuring those who trust us know that we are truly invested in their cause.

Don't wait for an award or a bouquet to be handed over to you. Trust me, no one's lining up with a garland and a slow clap. Please note you're not expecting any kind words from the donor. Appreciation is a rare species in this world. Most will only care whether you delivered what was promised, and whether you did it on time. Your job? Smile, nod, and assure them you will. And then… go back to refreshing that email for a reply that says nothing but at least, "Noted."

Get it. Got it. Good!

The Internal Universe:
The Secret to Getting Things Done

While donor relationships often take centre stage, there exists another world. It is one that is rarely spoken about but holds the true key to success. It's the internal universe. And in this universe, you are the nucleus.

Finance, Programmes, HR, Procurement, Communications. Each of these teams operates within its own orbit, governed by its own rules, timelines, and priorities. They have their own fires to put out, their own deliverables to chase. And then, there is you, carrying a donor requirement that feels like the most urgent thing in the world. But to them? It is just another task in an already overflowing to-do list.

Here's the reality: Your donor's work may not be their priority. Not because they don't care, but because their roles demand a different focus. So, how do you make sure your work gets done? How do you get that crucial report from Finance, that impact data from Programmes, that clearance from HR? The answer isn't force. It's friendship.

In the rush to meet deadlines and fulfil donor commitments, it is easy to assume that authority alone will move things forward. You might be tempted to march in like a commander, expecting things to happen simply because they should. After all, the work is important, the deadlines are real, and the pressure is mounting. But issuing demands like battle orders rarely wins the war.

Instead, step in with a flower, not a spear. You build allies, not adversaries. You learn what makes each department tick, what challenges they face, and you show empathy. The best way to get your work prioritised is to ensure that the person helping you feels valued. A request framed with empathy and respect often gets better results than one that feels forceful. Sometimes, collaboration, diplomacy sprinkled with respect, can be just as effective in comparison to the assertive 'get this done'. Both approaches may get the job done, but only one builds goodwill for the long run.

Think of it this way, if you have a friend in Finance, they won't just process your report; they'll make sure it gets done first. If you have a trusted ally in Communications, your donor update or the thank you note to your donor on social media won't just be another task; it will be something they genuinely want to perfect.

It's a secret few talk about, yet it's the ultimate game-changer. The internal world can be your biggest bottleneck or your greatest advantage. It all depends on how you navigate it and how you manage it. Never demand, always request. Never command, always stay humble.

And above all, remember what the Arabs said, *'keep the tongue sweet'*.

Navigating Internal Resistance: From Friction to Flow

Alright, player, let's be real. Not every department will be your biggest fan, and that is a reality you need to accept early on. As the front-facing representative, the bridge between donors and internal teams, you will often find yourself caught in the middle. And bridges? They bear the weight of both sides.

At times, the demands will pull you in opposite directions, stretching you so thin it feels like you've got elastic limbs straight out of a superhero comic.

When donor requirements come in, they come with urgent requests. Be it reports, funding clarifications, programme updates, etc. It is you who has to knock on multiple doors, push for responses, and ensure timely execution. This naturally creates friction. Some teams may see you as an outsider disrupting their workflow; someone might take it that you are bringing in more work rather than a shared purpose. And some might complain *'salah kitna pressure deytha hai' (The guy puts so much pressure)*. The first stage of your internal journey will be a slight pushback.

And here is where navigation matters. Instead of pushing harder and reinforcing resistance, you need to ease into the system. You cannot be a shark, charging ahead and expecting compliance. That will only deepen the divide. Instead, be the dolphin. One that swims with the group, moves with agility, and builds connections. Dolphins don't dominate; they collaborate. They are intelligent, playful, and trusted within their pods. That's exactly how you need to establish yourself as a player.

Listen to what internal teams need, understand their pain points, and show them that you are not just there to take, but instead you are there to partner. Over time, the resistance will ease, and you'll transform from an outsider into an essential connector in the organisation's ecosystem.

Beyond Work:
The Unexpected Role of a Workplace Confidant

When you spend enough time in an organisation, you start to notice something. You are always being watched. Not in an ominous way, but in the quiet, passing moments. Your colleagues observe you, forming their own silent verdicts. Some see you as dependable, others as indifferent. If you are lucky, you become "the nice person." And once a reputation settles in, word spreads whether you realise it or not.

Before long, you hear whispers of your name in conversations. *"You know, Wasif might have the answer to this."* Or, *"Maybe he doesn't."* And here is the surprising part. If they think you might, they will come to you. Not just for work, not just for deadlines, but for something far more personal.

It always starts the same way. A colleague lingers a little longer than usual, debating whether to speak. Then, almost hesitantly, they sit across from you, shifting in their seat before sharing something heavy: a personal crisis, a struggle they cannot quite voice to anyone else, a problem that no corporate handbook can solve. And that is when it hits you. You are no longer just a coworker. You have become something else. A confidant. A sounding board. A quiet source of comfort.

That is the real test. Not how well you close a deal, write a proposal, or navigate office politics, but how you show up for people when they need you most. The world's greatest relationship managers are not just good at winning donors. They understand people at their core.

And when that moment comes, when someone chooses *you* to be the person they turn to, be there. Listen. Offer wisdom where you can. Because long after the spreadsheets are forgotten and the projects are complete, these are the moments that will define you.

In the end, we do not just work with people. We grow with them. And that, more than anything, is what makes the journey worthwhile.

The Crash Course

1. Trust Is the Currency of Every Relationship

Whether you're managing million-dollar accounts, securing life-changing donations, or sweet-talking your neighbour into babysitting for free, trust is the bedrock of it all. People may sign cheques for institutions, but they stay loyal to people they trust. For any relationship manager (RM) or the organisation the RM represents, credibility isn't just an asset, it's the *only* asset that truly matters.

2. Master the Art of the Follow-Up

There's a thin line between a thoughtful reminder and a restraining order. The best follow-ups aren't about pestering; they're about nurturing relationships. Timing is everything. A well-placed check-in can make you unforgettable; relentless emails will make you unblockable (and not in a good way).

3. Donor Retention: The Real Trophy

Anyone can land a first gift. The real magic lies in securing the second, the third, and the tenth. A great RM knows that fundraising doesn't stop when the money arrives. The care you show between donations through timely updates, meaningful engagement, and genuine gratitude determines whether a donor becomes a lifelong supporter or a one-time blip on your database.

4. Every Interaction Is a Storytelling Opportunity

Data informs, but stories inspire. People don't open their hearts (or wallets) because of spreadsheets; they do it because they feel connected to a bigger purpose. Whether you're in a high-stakes pitch or a casual conversation, use stories to bring your cause to life.

5. Patience and Diplomacy: Your Secret Weapons

Fundraising is a world of personalities and not all of them play nice. Some donors want granular details; others communicate in vague riddles. A great RM navigates these complexities with calmness, clarity, and a talent for reading between the lines. Keep your cool and know when to push and when to pause.

6. Renewals: Silent but Powerful Victories

When a donor renews without hesitation, it's the ultimate vote of confidence. But renewals don't happen by accident. The work you do between donations delivering impact reports, offering personal updates, and responding promptly lays the foundation for a seamless yes. If your donors trust you to deliver, they'll keep showing up.

7. Referrals Are Gold Dust

A warm introduction from a trusted donor or even your board members can save you months of cold calls and ignored emails. While due diligence and follow-up conversations still apply, nothing accelerates a relationship like a credible referral. Treat every satisfied donor as a potential bridge to new opportunities.

8. Mastering the Internal Maze

Fundraising isn't just external; some of your biggest challenges (and wins) happen within your own organisation. Finance, Programmes, HR, Procurement, Communications – each department has its own priorities. To get things done, build relationships across these silos. Treat your internal colleagues with the same respect and care you extend to donors. And if all else fails, a well-timed box of samosas never hurts.

9. Becoming the Accidental Therapist

Relationship management often means wearing unexpected hats. One day, you're a strategist; the next, a shoulder to cry on. Whether it's guiding a donor through personal concerns or helping a colleague navigate workplace challenges, being a compassionate listener is an underrated superpower.

At its core, fundraising is not about asking for money; it's about building relationships strong enough that people *want* to give. Let's be real, donors won't remember your 10-slide impact presentation or that beautifully crafted email (which they probably skimmed), but they **will** remember how you made them feel.

Make a donor feel like a world-saving superhero? *Jackpot!*

Assuring the donor that you will not run away with the money? *Million-dollar lottery win!*

Make them feel like a confused hostage trapped in your pitch? *Better luck next time.*

Talking from the script? *"Thank you, try again!"*

Bottom line is master the art of making people feel valuable, and you're not just a fundraiser but on your way to becoming *The World's Greatest Relationship Manager* (cape and theme song sold separately). All it takes is the right mannerisms, persistence, and the ability to make people feel like billionaires - emotionally, at least. And yeah, if you can make someone *want* to take your call more than twice, congratulations! You might just be ready for your own action figure.

Truth Bytes

The Dignity Cold Call

I stared at the number on my screen. Another cold call. Another shot at securing funding. I exhaled, hit dial, and braced myself.

The line connected. A clipped voice answered. "Hello?"

I shared my name, the organisation I was calling from, and gave a quick overview of our mission.

There was an audible breath of impatience. "Look, I get these calls all the time. What do you want?"

I had two choices in that moment:

1. Push through with my scripted pitch and risk getting shut down.

2. Acknowledge the reality and shift my approach.

I chose the second.

Acknowledging his irritation, I expressed that I understood how frustrating cold calls could be. There was never an intention to take up his time unnecessarily. The outreach came from a place of genuine belief that the work we were doing aligned closely with his area of focus. If he was open to it, I would be glad to share a brief overview of our efforts and impact. And if he wasn't, that choice would be respected without any hesitation or pressure. Sometimes, just creating the space for someone to choose makes all the difference.

There was a pause. Then the tone softened. "Alright. Send me a brief. I'll take a look."

That was all I needed. No push. No desperation. Just a door left slightly open.

What I've learned is this: cold calling is not about volume. It is about intent. When done with care, it opens doors. When rushed or transactional, it closes them. A relentless, sales-driven approach strips fundraising of its soul, turning a heartfelt mission into just another pitch aimed at meeting a target.

We are not selling a product. We are advocating for change. The ask must be honest. The need must be genuine. And if you ever find yourself making a call just to tick a box on a target sheet, you know you need to pause and ask yourself why you are doing this in the first place.

Fundraising is not about delivering the perfect Shakespearean pitch either. It is about being real. No potential donor wants to talk to someone who sounds like a recorded script. So, ditch the jargon, keep it simple, and speak like a human!

At its core, it's not strategy or script. It's one human being connecting with another.

And yes, that turned out to be the last cold call I ever made. Truth be told, I was never really the cold-calling type to begin with.

Chapter 8

Emotional Intelligence of a Fundraiser

Honestly, when I first outlined this book and decided its chapters, the subject of emotional intelligence felt too soft and squishy, like something you'd find on a motivational GIF on a *Good Morning* WhatsApp message forwarded by one of your uncles. But the more time I spent reflecting (and reading), the more I realised that emotional intelligence isn't just a nice-to-have; it's actually a secret sauce that differentiates an average fundraiser from a superior one.

Behind every major gift and long-term donor relationship lies an intricate dance of emotions, empathy, and self-control. And let's face it, if you can't keep your cool when a donor asks for an extra impact report on a Friday night, this might not be the career for you.

What kind of character does it take to be a successful fundraiser? On the surface, it might seem like the job is all about numbers, meeting targets, securing commitments, and closing deals. But beneath the spreadsheets and polished presentations lies something far more profound: the character of the person doing the asking.

A fundraiser is, at its core, a bridge between those who have resources and those who need them. This unique position demands more than just persuasive speech or business acumen. It requires a finely tuned emotional intelligence. The ability to understand and navigate human emotions, both others' and one's own.

Emotional intelligence has a huge impact on how we work and who we become. The high performers we all admire often have one thing in common - a strong grasp of emotional intelligence. It all starts with being self-aware, and you'd better take note of that.

Think of emotional intelligence as a muscle. Over time, you develop the ability to recognise and understand the emotions within yourself and those around you. It is this ability that allows you to manage your behaviour and your relationships effectively. Plenty of books discuss emotional intelligence, but let's break it down in a way that applies directly to fundraising.

How Do You Apply It?

Our job is all about people, right? It is more about building genuine relationships than just making an ask. Trust doesn't happen overnight. It is earned through deeper connections and meaningful conversations. And here is the kicker: many factors determine whether a relationship flourishes or fizzles out. Sometimes, you are the reason it works. Other times, you are the reason it doesn't.

I remember my first day walking into the hallway of my MBA programme in Dubai. The place was buzzing. People from different nationalities were chatting away, flashing their latest gadgets. I clenched my fist tightly and wondered, "Will I fit in?" Was I wearing the right clothes? Would the cool inner circle accept me? It felt like a high-stakes social audition.

Guess what? Those feelings never completely disappear. Whether you are a banker, working in any service industry or as a fundraiser, or something else entirely, you will always wonder if you are saying the right words, wearing the right clothes, or doing it the right way. That self-doubt can throw you off track if you let it.

Here is the reality check: You can have all the operational knowledge and legal know-how in the world, but conflicting motivations will always test you. These competing motivations, whether it is your ambition versus a donor's hesitation or your deadlines versus their timing, can either derail you or push you to grow.

In fundraising, remember one golden rule: You are not just paid to talk. You are paid to listen as well.

Think more about them and less about yourself. Simple, right? But it is harder than it sounds. It takes real emotional intelligence to quiet your inner monologue and focus entirely on the person in front of you.

The "Secret Signals" Game

Sometimes, the most important things are left unsaid. Emotional intelligence means tuning in to those unspoken cues, a donor's body language, the hesitancy in their voice, or the momentary pause before they answer. I once met a donor who gave me a polite smile but kept their arms crossed the entire meeting. Had I bulldozed ahead with my pitch, I would have missed the discomfort behind that posture.

Instead, I pivoted. I asked an open-ended question: "What inspired you to consider supporting causes like ours?" That simple question cracked open the conversation. It turned out they had a deep personal connection to our work but worried whether their contribution would truly make a difference. By noticing the secret signals, I was able to address their concerns head-on.

There are some who are not even ready to switch on their cameras in a Teams call. I am wondering, I am here all decked up and the other person prefers the *parda (veil)*?

Eyes Don't Lie

If you want to know what someone is truly feeling, watch their eyes. Words can be rehearsed, smiles can be faked, but the eyes? They tell the truth. I once sat across from a donor who kept nodding enthusiastically at everything I said, but their eyes told a different story. There was a flicker of hesitation, a glimmer of doubt that no number of polished responses could hide.

I paused mid-pitch and said, "I get the sense that you have some reservations. What's on your mind?" That moment of honesty shifted everything. They admitted they had been burned by a previous non-profit that promised impact but delivered excuses. That simple acknowledgement gave me the opening to address their fears transparently. By trusting what I saw rather than just what I heard, I was able to salvage a conversation that could have easily slipped away.

When you learn to read the eyes, you unlock a new layer of communication. It is not just about the words spoken; it is about the fears, hopes, and questions hidden beneath them. As a fundraiser, understanding those unspoken truths can be the difference between closing a gift and losing a donor's trust.

When Diplomacy Turns into a Performance

Every fundraiser has faced the over-diplomatic type, the ones who float into a room with a carefully rehearsed smile and a tone dripping with polished charm. They speak in circles, never quite revealing their true intentions, while making sure everyone knows they are the smartest person in the room. At first glance, they seem untouchable. But look closer, and you will see the cracks.

I once met a corporate executive who embodied this persona perfectly. From the moment we sat down, he spoke in vague, polished statements, hinting at his "deep commitment" to social causes while subtly reminding me how busy and important he was. I knew this wasn't going to be a straightforward conversation. Rather than get caught in his performance, I asked him one simple question: "What keeps you up at night?"

His demeanour shifted. The mask slipped, just a little. He leaned back, paused, and for the first time, his words weren't rehearsed. He shared concerns about the legacy he wanted to leave behind. That one honest answer changed the entire dynamic. Suddenly, we were two people having a real conversation and not a performance.

When faced with over-diplomatic personalities, emotional intelligence means cutting through the act without calling it out. Ask the right questions. Give them space to drop the mask. People want to be understood beneath their polished exteriors, and when you meet them there, you build something real.

As for others who are too good at wearing the mask and not dropping it, leave it there and move on.

The Art of Difficult Conversations

Let's be honest, not everyone you work with will have a high emotional IQ. Some donors will be demanding, dismissive, or downright rude. The trick is not to mirror their energy. Emotional intelligence means choosing your response when others are losing their cool.

Fundraising isn't always sunshine and smooth sailing. Sometimes you have to navigate tricky waters, like when a donor has unrealistic expectations or when a long-standing supporter starts to pull back. Emotional intelligence is what keeps you from reacting impulsively.

I once had a donor who insisted on controlling every aspect of a project they funded, down to the font size on our reports. Every update felt like walking on eggshells. Instead of pushing back immediately, I took a different route. I invited them to visit our campus. Seeing the work firsthand shifted their perspective from control to collaboration. Emotional intelligence means recognising when to speak and when to let experiences speak for themselves. If they insist on it, then understand where they are coming from and gift them their requirements accordingly. No point crying over spilt milk.

What Experience Teaches That Books Don't

When in doubt, make it about them. When you focus on the donor's motivations, emotions, and goals, you move from a salesperson to a trusted advisor. And that's where real magic happens.

1. **Practice active listening**: Focus on what the donor is saying without preparing your next response.

2. **Manage your triggers**: Identify situations that make you defensive and develop strategies to stay calm.

3. **Read between the lines**: Pay attention to non-verbal cues and underlying concerns.

4. **Stay curious**: Ask thoughtful questions that reveal a donor's deeper motivations.

5. **Lead with empathy**: Remember, fundraising is about people first, always.

The Heart Behind the Ask

Emotional intelligence transforms fundraising from a transactional hustle into a human-centred art. It is the difference between making an ask and building a relationship. When you understand your own emotions and those of your donors, you stop being just a fundraiser. You become a trusted partner in something bigger.

The Ethics of a Fundraiser

Emotional intelligence without ethics is like a compass without true north. Fundraisers hold a profound responsibility not just to their organisations but to their donors and the communities they serve. Ethical fundraising is the bedrock of lasting relationships and sustainable impact. It means being honest, transparent, and respecting the dignity of all parties involved.

Be Truthful and Transparent

Always tell the truth about your organisation's work and the impact of a donor's contribution. Avoid exaggerating outcomes, fabricating stories, or making promises you cannot keep. Honesty fosters trust, and trust is the foundation of every successful fundraising relationship. When you present the facts clearly, even when they reveal challenges or setbacks, you invite donors to become true partners in your mission. Misrepresentation, however small, risks undermining the very cause you seek to advance.

Transparency also means being upfront about how funds will be used. Provide clear, detailed breakdowns of programme costs and demonstrate how donor contributions translate into tangible outcomes. When donors understand where their money goes, they are more likely to continue supporting your cause. If there are limitations or uncertainties, address them openly rather than leaving room for misunderstandings.

Respect Donor Privacy

Donor relationships are built on trust, and trust requires safeguarding personal information. Handle sensitive data with care and discretion, ensuring compliance with legal standards and ethical best practices. Confidentiality is not just a regulatory requirement; it is a moral commitment.

Be clear about how you collect, store, and use donor information. Obtain explicit consent before sharing any personal data and provide donors with the option to remain anonymous if they wish. Mishandling donor information can irreparably damage your reputation and break the bond of trust you work so hard to build.

Honour Donor Intent

Respecting donor intent is a cornerstone of ethical fundraising. When someone gives, they do so with a purpose in mind. It is your responsibility to ensure their contribution is used in alignment with their wishes and your organisation's mission.

Be diligent in documenting donor preferences and communicating how their support directly advances the cause they care about. If circumstances require a change in how funds are allocated, inform donors promptly and seek their approval when possible. Ignoring donor intent risks alienating supporters and jeopardising future giving.

Avoid Conflicts of Interest

Integrity demands that fundraisers place the mission above personal gain or external pressures. Be vigilant in identifying and addressing potential conflicts of interest. This means disclosing any relationships or financial interests that could influence your professional judgement.

When faced with ethical dilemmas, prioritise the best interests of the communities you serve and the donors who trust you. If a situation could create even the appearance of impropriety, address it transparently and seek guidance from organisational leadership or ethics committees when necessary.

Cultivate a Culture of Ethics

Ethical fundraising is not an individual responsibility; it is a collective commitment. Organisations should establish clear ethical guidelines and provide regular training to ensure all staff and volunteers uphold these principles.

Create systems for accountability and encourage open dialogue about ethical concerns. A culture that values ethics strengthens internal morale and reinforces your public credibility. By holding yourself and your organisation to the highest ethical standards, you not only protect your mission but also set an example for the broader philanthropic community.

The Long Game of Integrity

In fundraising, success is measured not just by the dollars you raise but by the trust you sustain. Ethical lapses may yield short-term gains but inevitably erode long-term relationships. By anchoring your work in honesty, respect, and integrity, you build a legacy that extends far beyond any single campaign or contribution.

When faced with difficult choices, remember that your duty is to the truth and to the people you serve. Ethical fundraising is not simply a professional obligation; it is a moral calling that shapes the world you wish to create.

Truth Bytes

The Donor's Dog Barked First

Sometimes, you'll be halfway through your pitch when a donor's dog barks louder than your voice. And guess what? That bark gets more attention than your entire proposal.

Moral?

You're not just pitching to people. You're pitching to their lives, their distractions, their pets, and their inbox full of better offers.

So, what do you do?

Simply Adapt.

Enough said!

Chapter 9

Power of Volunteering in Fundraising

Volunteering is a sacred space where it all begins. It is the bridge between intent and impact, between awareness and action. It is here that individuals not only contribute but also transform, growing from casual supporters into dedicated champions of a cause. For fundraisers, harnessing the power of volunteerism is not just a strategy, it is a pathway to building relationships that endure beyond a single donation.

Volunteering provides firsthand exposure to an organisation's mission, operations, and impact, fostering a deep emotional connection that often transforms volunteers into passionate advocates and lifelong donors. Engaging at the grassroots level instils a sense of ownership and commitment, making volunteers more likely to contribute financially or introduce valuable networks. Additionally, volunteering offers aspiring fundraisers essential skills such as relationship-building, storytelling, and donor stewardship that form the foundation of successful fundraising efforts. In many cases, today's volunteers become tomorrow's most dedicated supporters, making volunteer engagement a strategic pillar in long-term fundraising success.

The transition from volunteer to donor is not just possible, it is a natural progression when nurtured correctly. A volunteer who spends time immersed in a cause develops an emotional stake in its success. They do not just witness change, they become part of it. And when people feel a sense of belonging, their willingness to give, whether time, expertise, or financial resources, becomes second nature.

From a fundraiser's perspective, the true beauty of volunteering lies in its potential for sustained engagement. Volunteers who dedicate their time gain an insider's understanding of an organisation's challenges and victories. This firsthand experience cultivates empathy, fostering a deep-rooted sense of responsibility. More importantly, because their connection is built on personal experience rather than obligation, their support tends to be enduring and impactful. Yes, personal experience is the key.

The shift from volunteer to donor happens most naturally when nurtured with care. Effective fundraisers recognise every volunteer interaction as an opportunity to inspire future giving. Simple gestures such as publicly acknowledging contributions, sharing impact stories, and inviting volunteers to exclusive events reinforce their emotional bond with the cause. Over time, these touchpoints transform volunteers into financial supporters who not only give but also champion the mission within their circles.

From Volunteers to Visionary Partners: A Journey of Commitment

When a corporate partner from the medical field first reached out to us, it seemed like a routine CSR inquiry.

Their organisation had a well-established Corporate Social Responsibility initiative and was constantly exploring meaningful engagement opportunities. During their research, they came across our work and scheduled a standard site visit, one of many they conducted throughout the year.

But from the moment their team stepped onto our site, something shifted. What was supposed to be a formal assessment quickly turned into a powerful emotional experience. What captivated them was the energy, the passion, and the undeniable impact they witnessed firsthand. They arrived as observers but left as believers.

The Volunteer Phase: Building Bonds Beyond Transactions

Rather than jumping into financial commitments, the corporate team chose a different path. They started by volunteering. Over the next three years, employees from different teams within the company visited us annually. They rolled up their sleeves and actively participated in a variety of activities. No money exchanged hands during this period, only time, effort, and a genuine connection.

Each visit strengthened their bond with our mission. The more they engaged, the more they saw the impact of their work. The more impact was seen, the more of the senior leadership started the visits. The enthusiasm was contagious. Soon, different departments within the company began expressing interest in joining the initiative. Employees became our biggest cheerleaders, championing our cause within their corporate ecosystem.

What started as a single visit soon turned into multiple engagements, each one deepening their connection to our cause. The initial curiosity led to a second visit, then a third, until it became an annual tradition within the company. As different teams took part, word spread internally, and enthusiasm grew.

The Turning Point: A Call That Changed Everything

Then came the day that transformed this partnership forever. My phone rang, and on the other end was one of their senior CSR heads. The voice carried a tone of both pride and purpose.

"We have volunteered on visits in the past, so this time we thought we should contribute to funding."

That moment marked a turning point. The years of volunteering had built trust, authenticity, and an unshakeable emotional investment in our cause. They were no longer just contributors of time. They were ready to commit financially. A comprehensive proposal was drafted for a two-year support period, and it was approved without hesitation. The decision felt natural, even inevitable, the result of years of authentic engagement rather than a transactional request.

The Quiet Catalyst: A Volunteer's Gift

One of the most memorable transformations I have witnessed began with a volunteer who, at first glance, seemed an unlikely champion. He was a college intern, dark-eyed, slightly awkward, often juggling textbooks under one arm. His task was simple: manage spreadsheets and gather email addresses of executives from annual reports. But there was something about him. He showed up without fail, asked thoughtful questions about the fundraising landscape, and unknowingly became an integral part of my daily rhythm.

One afternoon, during our usual Teams call, he overheard me speaking with a colleague about a COVID project that had stalled due to a lack of funding. It was the kind of initiative that tugged at our hearts but had reached a financial block. He paused and said, "I know someone who might help." I assumed it was a classmate or a professor. To my surprise, it was his father, the CEO of a major corporation.

Two weeks later, my CEO and I were presenting our vision on a Teams call to a room full of senior executives. It was the sort of meeting fundraisers dream of, with engaged decision-makers who had the power to turn bold ideas into reality. That quiet intern, with his unassuming nature and unexpected connection, opened a door that led to a corporate partnership. The support that followed filled critical gaps at a time when others remained silent. During the peak of the COVID crisis, when most wouldn't take calls or respond to emails, he stepped up and made sure we were heard.

The lesson is simple yet profound. Never underestimate those who show up. Sometimes, the most reserved volunteers carry within them the keys to extraordinary possibilities. When you treat each person like they matter, you might just discover an ally in the most unexpected of places.

At its heart, fundraising is about showing up again and again with a sense of purpose. It is like stepping onto a stage each day. You gather yourself, wear your invisible makeup, rehearse your lines, and remind yourself why you do what you do. Some days, the spotlight feels warm and encouraging. Other days, it feels like no one is watching. But you still show up.

Every call you make and every meeting you walk into holds the possibility of changing someone's mind or opening a new door. It is not just about helping the people you serve. It is also about inspiring those who have the power to help. In this space filled with emotions, uncertainty, and countless unanswered emails, the ones who make it are those who keep going. They know that every no could be one step closer to a yes. They believe that even the smallest gesture, a kind word, a shared story, a single connection, can spark something much bigger than they imagined.

In fundraising, magic often hides in the most unexpected places.

Champions of Change:
How Giving Transformed into a Movement

It began with an invitation from a multinational bank. An institution known not just for its global reach, but for its deep commitment to meaningful change. They had been following our work, quietly observing the lives we were changing and the communities we were uplifting. When they finally reached out, their message was clear: *We want to do more.*

What followed was not a standard CSR conversation. They did not just want to support a cause. They wanted to create a lasting impact. They wanted to go beyond the cheque and build something that would inspire their people from within. They asked, *How can we make our employees a part of this journey? How do we help them not just contribute, but lead?*

We met. We listened. We dreamed together. And out of those early conversations, a powerful idea emerged: to turn employees into champions. Not only as donors, but also as storytellers, advocates, and believers in the mission.

And so, we gave them the stage.

What began with a few teams in India learning about our work soon spread across borders. Employees from different departments, offices, and countries across the Asia-Pacific region began to rally behind the cause. They started small fundraisers during lunch breaks, birthday pledges, office challenges, sports Olympiads, and charity runs. What seemed modest at first quickly gained momentum.

This was not about any grand gestures. It was about consistency. It was about people showing up, doing what they could, and inspiring others to do the same. Bit by bit, they built something powerful together.

And then came the turning point. The bank saw what was happening. This was no longer just a CSR initiative. It had become a movement driven by their own people. In response, leadership stepped forward and made a bold commitment. The bank matched every rupee raised by employees. One effort became two. Each gesture turned into a ripple.

Year after year, the numbers grew. But more importantly, so did the sense of ownership. The employees were no longer just supporting a cause. They were shaping it.

And that, my dear reader, is the true power of fundraising. Not just money raised, but people moved. Not just donations given, but lives transformed. It does not just become a success story; it is a legacy. And it is still being written.

The next story? Who knows... it could be yours.

Truth Bytes

What My Son Taught Me

The evening air buzzed with the chatter of families, the hum of arcade machines, and the distant clatter of trays in the food court. My eight-year-old son and I had just wrapped up our weekly arcade visit, a ritual he cherished. He had mastered the art of stretching his tokens to the last possible game, strategising every move to maximise his rewards. Now, as we sat at a corner table in the food court, silence settled between us. He was busy with his fries, methodically picking each one while the rest of his meal lay forgotten. I sat across from him, sipping water, waiting for my food from another outlet.

Something in me snapped.

I don't know why, but I picked a fight. Maybe it was the exhaustion from the week, maybe it was a lingering frustration, or maybe it was something I wasn't ready to admit to myself. The day before, he had made a phone call. He had reached out to someone, let's call him Mr. X, and asked him for a favour. Without hesitation, without consideration, X had said no. A blunt, sharp, emotionless no, with some more things to say. Coincidentally, my son had kept the phone on speaker and I overheard the conversation from the other room, and it sent a wave of anger through me.

And so, in that moment, in the middle of that crowded food court, I decided to teach my son a lesson.

"The world is not a great place," I told him. "It's not filled with great people. You need to stop trusting so easily. People don't care about your feelings. You have to be strong. You can't be this vulnerable." My words came out harsh, laced with a bitterness I hadn't intended. I kept going. "You should never have called. See what X did? He doesn't care. Why did you even reach out? Don't ever talk to him again."

My son stopped eating.

Slowly, deliberately, he put his fries down. Then he looked up, straight into my eyes. His voice was soft, yet it carried a weight that silenced everything around us. He slowly spoke.

"But Daddy, we have a relationship with X. We can't just end it."

I felt something shift inside me. The world around me faded. The arcade sounds, the chatter, the clatter of dishes, all of it blurred into insignificance. My mind and heart stood still, paralysed by an eight-year-old's truth.

This wasn't a child who lived in a bubble. He had seen the world, faced its shadows. He wasn't growing up in the protected corridors of a utopian school where every lesson was curated to shape him into a model citizen. He had already faced rejection, already seen glimpses of bullying, hate and exclusion. And yet, here he was, holding on to something pure, something I had lost sight of thanks to the perils of society.

In that moment, it felt as if my soul had stepped outside my body, turned to face me, and placed a finger on my lips. A silent command. A verdict passed not from an elder to a child, but from a child to his father.

Keep the relationship.

I had no right to argue. No right to teach a lesson I didn't fully understand myself. Relationships weren't about the momentary stings of rejection or the fleeting hurts of indifference. They were built on something deeper, something resilient, something that even an eight-year-old knew to protect.

And maybe, just maybe, that is what fundraising is too!

We reach out. Sometimes, we hear a blunt no. Sometimes, silence is all we get in return. But relationships aren't about a single call, a single ask, a single moment. They are nurtured over time. They are fought for, protected, and honoured, even when the answer is not what we want to hear.

That evening, as my son returned to his fries, my thoughts drifted into unfamiliar territory. The lesson I had intended to teach had circled back to me, reshaped and far more profound than I had imagined.

Keep the relationship. Always.

Because sometimes, the strongest bonds are not built on yeses but on the persistence that follows a no.

And yet, I find myself still thinking, still questioning. Perhaps some lessons are not meant to be neatly resolved or immediately understood. Perhaps they simply linger, unfolding at their own slow pace.

Chapter 10

Beyond The Giving

———— ·◆· ————

We've reached the final chapter. But while these may be the last pages of the book, it's far from the end of the story. I hope this journey has ignited something within you, a deeper understanding of fundraising, perhaps a renewed sense of purpose, or even the curiosity to explore this world further.

Before I became a fundraiser, I was a student of social development management at a premier institute. As part of the curriculum, I undertook a nine-month research project with a small but dedicated NGO, which I selected at the start of the course. What began as an academic requirement soon turned into a transformative experience, offering me deep insights into the non-profit world.

I witnessed the quiet yet profound power of gratitude, the far-reaching impact of prosocial behaviour, and the significance of intangible benefits. These lessons were more than just observations; they became the foundation of my approach to fundraising. My research not only shaped my understanding but also prepared me for the path ahead.

Here is what I learned.

Fundraising is often seen as a transactional process, an exchange of money for impact. However, those who truly understand it know that fundraising is not just about securing funds; it is about building relationships. At the core of every lasting donor connection lies something far more valuable than money: gratitude. This realisation led me to develop the concept of the 'Gratitude Cycle', a powerful force that fuels sustained giving and deeper engagement.

In this chapter, let's explore the psychology of gratitude, the unseen benefits that drive generosity, and how fundraisers can harness this cycle to cultivate long-term donor commitment. The focus is on individual givers, the true champions of philanthropy.

A Walk Towards a Life-Changing Realisation

During my research days, I travelled daily to this humble NGO tucked away in Worli, Mumbai. My journey began at Andheri railway station, where I would board a local train, squeezing into the crowded second-class compartment. It was a world apart from the smooth, air-conditioned comfort of the Dubai Metro, where I once commuted alongside my dearest Filipino colleagues. That life had been familiar, but I embraced the change. The chaotic rush, the rhythmic clatter of train wheels, and the vendors calling out their wares were all part of my initiation into Mumbai's lifeblood. I felt a deep respect for the city and its relentless energy.

As the train pulled into Mahalaxmi station, I stepped onto the platform, thinking my journey was almost over. But the NGO was not in Mahalaxmi; it was farther away in

Worli. Cabs were scarce, and I had neither the patience to wait for a bus. So, I walked.

And what a walk it was.

The path from Mahalaxmi to Worli led me through the serene corridors of the Mahalaxmi Racecourse, a stunning contrast between two worlds. On one side, Mumbai's ever-rising skyline pierced the sky, with concrete and steel stretching toward infinity. On the other, a short but beautiful stretch of lush green remained untouched by the urban chaos, a tranquil haven amidst the city's restless pace. That 20-minute walk became a ritual, an unexpected moment of calm before I stepped into the intense and emotional world of my research.

I was there to conduct in-depth qualitative interviews with beneficiaries, to hear their stories firsthand, and to understand the depth of impact this small yet powerful NGO had on individual lives. But what I discovered was more than just research material. It was a revelation, one that would forever shape the way I understood fundraising.

As I used to reach the doorstep of the NGO each day, a few beneficiaries would already be waiting for their interviews with me. The CEO had thoughtfully arranged for them to come to the office, ensuring I had the space I needed to conduct my sessions. It was a kind gesture that I appreciated throughout my time there.

Each time, I stood at the threshold of this experience with no prior background in the field. Taking a deep breath, I would steady myself and step forward, ready to begin.

A Mother's Unwavering Strength:
The Story That Changed Everything

One of the most unforgettable stories I encountered during these interview sessions was that of a mother and her daughter who had fought the battle against kidney cancer. Seventeen years before 2018, this mother had approached this NGO in search of help. Her daughter, now an adult and a cancer survivor living with just one kidney, remains deeply connected to the organisation that once saved her life.

She recalled the desperation of those days. Initially, she had gone to Tata Memorial Hospital in Mumbai, a place that is more than just a medical facility. It is a sanctuary of hope for thousands who arrive each day carrying nothing but faith and the weight of their struggles. Nestled in the heart of Mumbai, this institution has become a lifeline for the poor, offering world-class cancer treatment regardless of financial standing.

Walking through its doors, one can witness the pulse of rural India beating within its walls. The lobby is a sea of *waiting families, some perched on the floor, some huddled together in silent prayers, others clutching documents as if holding onto life itself.* The corridors stretch endlessly, lined with weary but resolute faces from every corner of the country. Farmers, labourers, mothers, fathers, and children stand together, bound by a common hope.

The staircases are never empty. They are filled with people navigating their way through this labyrinth of care, often barefoot, often exhausted, but always determined.

Language, caste, and status dissolve in this place. Everyone is equal in their suffering and in the compassion they receive. Doctors and nurses move tirelessly, embodying a quiet resilience, treating not just a disease but the despair that accompanies it. Tata Memorial is not just a place of medicine. It is a testament to human endurance, a reminder that even in the face of illness and adversity, kindness and healing prevail. Amidst the chaos, miracles happen every day. And yes, there are many such hospitals alike in India today.

At the hospital, a kind social worker directed the mother towards an NGO *(The same NGO where I am taking the interviews…)* known for funding life-saving treatments. With nothing but hope, she took a bus straight to the NGO's office and met the point of contact, who assured her, "We will help, no matter what it takes." And they did. Years of treatment, unwavering support, and relentless effort helped her daughter survive.

As she spoke, her strong, resilient frame stood out, a woman built for survival, both physically and mentally. Her voice carried no sadness, no victimhood, only determination, gratitude, and an unshakeable bond with the NGO that had stood by her side. Even today, she says, she has no one else to turn to apart from this organisation.

Life after survival has not been easy. Her daughter, now an adult, struggles with physical weakness due to the aggressive treatment she underwent as a child. She cannot work because of her fragile stamina. The family lives in a small hut by the sea at Worli, where every monsoon threatens to wash away their home.

Yet, the mother fights on. At 4:30 am in the wee hours of the morning, as the high tide retreats, she rushes to the shoreline to collect discarded scraps, plastic bottles, metal pieces, anything of value that the ocean brings to the shore. She sells these to the scrap dealer, her only source of income for the day. Her arms, strong from years of toil, are evidence of her resilience. But she does not complain. She does not seek sympathy. She only survives.

Even today, she remains deeply connected to the NGO, grateful for even the smallest gestures: an umbrella, used clothes, a few days' worth of rations. She knows that many NGOs have shut down, that survival is a daily struggle for families like hers. But as long as this NGO exists, she has hope. This NGO too has lost its strength and is not the strong NGO it once was, funded by HNIs at one point in time. This NGO too has its struggles and has shrunk its operations. The mother is aware but won't let go. Hope remains for both.

Her words still echo in my mind: *"Marthay dam tak main yahan aana chahti hoon"* (*Until my last breath, I want to keep coming here.*)

I remember this story vividly, and every time it comes to mind, I find myself whispering, *Wow.* In fact, the first time I heard it, I was completely mesmerised, I became a broken record, just sitting there nodding and going, *"Wow... Wow... Wow!"* If there were a contest for the most wows in a single conversation, I'd have won it right there!

Now, fast forward to me landing a job as a fundraiser. Exciting, right? Well, not so much really. I finally got a job after going off the grid for more than two years. I was almost broke when HR called me and said, "When can you join us?" Right in the middle of my *yay-I-have-a-job* moment, a tiny, nagging thought crept in: *Wait a minute... can these incredible stories, the unforgettable encounters with those unstoppable, rock-solid women of resilience during my research, actually help me in this role?* Only time will tell.

I realised on the job that fundraising had its own set of metrics, strategies, and that dreadful, ugly word: *targets*. It was all about numbers, pitches, polished presentations and the dreadful, endless documentation followed by reports. Sheets kept multiplying. But deep down, I couldn't shake the feeling that something bigger was at play, something beyond spreadsheets and impact reports. Could these raw, real, deeply human experiences hold the key to a fundraising philosophy that actually worked?

And then it hit me.

I was no longer a researcher taking notes. Now, I had to ask people for money. Convince them to give. Build relationships. And somewhere between my 'Oh no, what have I gotten myself into?' moment and my 'I should probably look like I know what I'm doing' phase, a tiny flicker of realisation sparked in my mind.

That flicker wasn't instant. Oh no. This wasn't some lightbulb moment. It was years in the making. Slow, gruelling, forehead-against-the-desk kind of years. Yet, piece by piece, the puzzle started coming together.

That mother's story, and the many others I had heard, wasn't just heartwarming. It was a key. Their gratitude wasn't just a polite 'thank you'. It was a force, a loop, a never-ending cycle of giving and receiving, of support and impact.

And then, there it was - *BAM!* The *Gratitude Cycle* was born.

Okay, fine, maybe not *Bam!* Exactly. More like *hmm... wait... hold on... oh! This actually makes sense, man!* But you get the idea.

Let's explore, shall we?

The Fundraising Gratitude Cycle

1. **Values:** The donor's belief system and motivation to give.

2. **Competency:** The fundraiser's ability to nurture and communicate impact.

3. **Intangible Benefits:** The emotional fulfilment donors receive from giving.

4. **Gratitude:** The driving force that renews and strengthens donor relationships.

Each of these elements fuels the next, creating a **powerful cycle of engagement and giving.**

THE FUNDRAISING GRATITUDE CYCLE

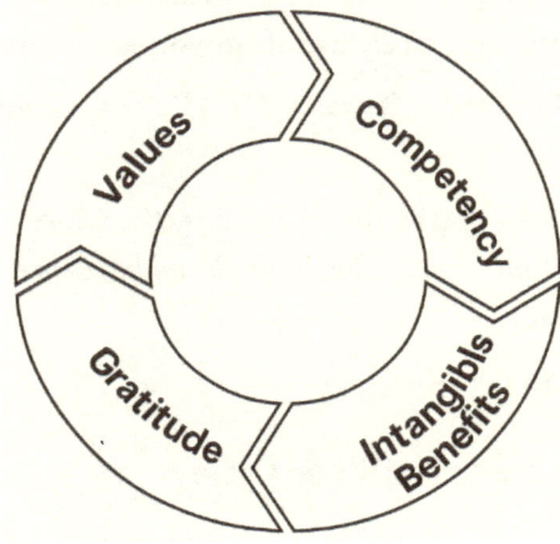

1. **Values: The core driver of individual giving**

   Why do people give? The motivations range from personal experiences and family traditions to religious faith and a sense of moral duty. Yet, at the heart of all individual philanthropy is a shared foundation of values. Donors seek to shape a world that reflects their beliefs, and fundraising is the bridge that connects their ideals to meaningful causes.

   However, values alone don't sustain giving; they need reinforcement. This is where fundraisers play a crucial role.

2. **Competency: The fundraiser's role in strengthening individual donor commitment**

   A true fundraiser is not just any salesperson; they are a relationship builder. If you want to keep it simple, you can call it a sales job in the non-profit world. But to elevate the role and create an exceptional experience, success isn't measured by how much they raise but by how effectively they engage, educate, and inspire the donors.

This means:

- Understanding a donor's values and motivations.
- Communicating impact effectively through compelling storytelling.
- Ensuring transparency and accountability in every interaction.

The more competent a fundraiser is, the more trust they build. And trust leads to deeper relationships, paving the way for the next phase of the cycle.

3. Intangible benefits: The real reward of giving

While some do, there are individual donors who do not give solely for recognition or tax benefits. The real reason they continue giving lies in something intangible: the emotional satisfaction of making a difference.

- The feeling of purpose that comes from supporting a cause.
- The sense of connection with a community or a movement.
- The fulfilment of seeing a real-world impact unfold because of their contributions.

Fundraisers often underestimate this aspect. But when donors feel emotionally invested, giving becomes an extension of their identity, not just a financial decision. *Yup, note that.*

4. Gratitude: The catalyst for sustained giving

Gratitude isn't just a 'thank you' note at the end of a campaign. It's the lifeblood of donor retention.

When an individual donor is genuinely appreciated, he or she experiences:

- A heightened sense of social worth (knowing their contribution matters).

- A stronger connection to the organisation (feeling like part of something bigger).

- A motivation to give again (seeing their values reflected in the impact).

This, in turn, reinforces their values, strengthens their bond with the fundraiser, and fuels another cycle of giving. Thus, gratitude is no longer just an emotion; it becomes a deeply respected strategy.

Practical Strategies for Fundraisers Engaging Individual Donors

If gratitude is so powerful, how can fundraisers intentionally use it to build stronger individual donor relationships?

1. **Go beyond the receipt:** A transactional acknowledgement isn't enough. Send personalised impact updates, handwritten notes, or even a video message, if possible.

2. **Make gratitude two-way:** Invite donors to events where they can interact with beneficiaries. Let them witness the impact firsthand.

3. **Recognise small gifts as big wins:** An INR 1000 donor today could be an INR 100,000 donor tomorrow if they feel valued.

4. **Celebrate donor milestones:** Acknowledge anniversaries of their first gift, recurring donations, or specific milestones they helped achieve.

5. **Encourage gratitude from beneficiaries:** Hearing directly from those impacted creates a powerful emotional connection.

For smaller NGOs, these strategies may seem overwhelming, but even gentle gestures of gratitude within your capacity can go a long way in strengthening donor relationships.

For the research, I was fortunate to be guided by the incredible Ms. Chandrika Parmar, my amazing research guide at the institute. She had a remarkable ability to sense where I was coming from, someone raw, new to the field, and still finding my footing. With her characteristic patience and sharp insight, she kept a close watch on my progress and constantly encouraged me to dig deeper, think harder, and stay grounded. Despite her packed schedule and the constant demands on her time, she was always available when I needed her guidance. Her presence and support became a quiet but powerful force behind the work I was doing. I still keep in touch with her now and then, and through this book, I want to take a moment to send her my heartfelt thanks and warmest wishes. Her belief in my research made all the difference.

If there's a teacher, professor, or mentor in your life who helped shape your path, no matter how long ago, go ahead and take a moment to thank them. Gratitude has a way of completing the story.

The Secret Ingredient of Successful Individual Giving

At its core, fundraising isn't just about securing donations. It is about cultivating a culture of gratitude. When appreciation is embedded in every interaction, it creates a ripple effect, enriching not just donors but also fundraisers and the lives they aim to change.

The true essence of a fundraiser's work goes beyond the ask. It is about ensuring that every individual donor feels seen, valued, and inspired. When that happens, fundraising transcends mere transactions and transforms into something far more powerful: an enduring cycle of generosity that continues long after the first gift is made.

First Keynote on Fundraising

The first time you do something truly significant in your fundraising journey, it tends to stay with you. Not just for what you did, but for what it meant. One such moment could be your very first keynote address. And when it comes, it won't just be another event on your calendar. It will be a milestone that reflects your growth, your grit, and the stories you've collected along the way.

Imagine standing in front of a room full of distinguished professionals, maybe doctors, educators, or corporate leaders. There's excitement, a touch of nerves, but above all, a sense of purpose. You're not there just to speak. You're there to inspire, to connect, and to invite people into the incredible world of impact and giving.

By the way, this was my first setting.

Now imagine if that opportunity comes your way, embrace it. Prepare for it with your heart. Because you never know who's listening and how your words might spark the next big act of generosity.

Here was my script for my first keynote. Go ahead, make the most of it.

A Very Good Morning, Ladies and Gentlemen, thank you for being here!

I am Wasif Hani, and I sincerely appreciate this opportunity to share insights on fundraising with all of you.

Fundraising is a subject that interests all of us in the non-profit sector. I am not a superstar fundraiser who instantly secures millions in donations. I am someone who stands in line, waits for my turn, starts conversations, builds relationships, and gradually converts potential supporters into donors. Today, my talk won't follow a linear format. Instead, I will share key insights from the field of fundraising, which I hope will be useful to you.

Understanding the Sources of Fundraising

Fundraising primarily comes from five major sources:

1. ***Corporate Social Responsibility (CSR):*** *As you know, companies allocate 2% of their profits to social causes. This is a significant funding source for non-profits.*

2. ***Foundations:*** *Many philanthropic foundations, both in India and abroad, focus on solving specific problems. These include organisations such as Azim Premji Foundation and Bill & Melinda Gates Foundation.*

3. ***High Net-Worth Individuals (HNIs):*** *These are individuals with substantial wealth who are interested*

in philanthropy. The key to securing their support is to ask, because unless you ask, you won't know their intent to give.

4. ***Retail Donations:*** *Individual giving, largely facilitated online, is a growing and essential component of fundraising.*

5. ***Facilitators & Aggregators:*** *Many platforms act as intermediaries connecting corporates with non-profits. Today, being in their good books is crucial for securing funding.*

Restricted vs. Unrestricted Funding

Fundraising can be categorised into two types:

- ***Restricted Funding:*** *Includes CSR and foundation grants, which are designated for specific programmes.*

- ***Unrestricted Funding:*** *Includes retail donations and HNI contributions, which provide flexibility to cover operational and administrative expenses. Having a balance of both is crucial for long-term sustainability.*

The Scale of Philanthropy in India

Given this distribution, non-profits must diversify their funding sources rather than relying solely on one category, such as CSR. Regulatory changes can significantly impact fundraising, making it crucial to adopt a well-rounded approach.

Steps in Fundraising:
No Rocket Science, Just Smart Work

Successful fundraising is not about a secret formula; it's about:

- Understanding your non-profit's sector

- Conducting thorough research

- Using good internet resources and networking

- Having the patience and persistence to build relationships

In my journey, I have learned that three key aspects drive fundraising success:

1. **Research:** Great research leads to great success. Understanding which companies and individuals align with your cause is essential. Follow them on LinkedIn and Twitter to track their interests and potential funding opportunities.

2. **Lead Generation:** Your organisation's board members should play a crucial role in helping fundraisers secure leads. They have access to influential networks and can provide key introductions.

3. **Proposal Writing:** A well-crafted, concise proposal is vital. A document outlining your non-profit's vision, impact, and sustainability plan is far more effective than an overly detailed, unfocused report.

Building Relationships and Engaging Stakeholders

Fundraising is as much about relationships as it is about financial transactions. Here are some effective strategies:

- ***Crowdfunding Platforms:*** *These websites can help raise funds while reducing fundraising costs.*

- ***Employee Engagement:*** *Some corporates may not have funds but are willing to contribute through employee volunteer programmes. This engagement fosters long-term relationships, leading to future donations.*

- ***Matching Grants:*** *Some companies match their employees' donations, doubling the impact. This is a growing trend in the Indian fundraising landscape.*

The Secret Ingredients to Fundraising Success

1. ***Storytelling:*** *Don't sell guilt. Instead, tell compelling stories that donors can emotionally connect with and remember.*

2. ***Persistence:*** *My CEO often says, "The harder you try, the luckier you get." Fundraising requires perseverance.*

3. ***Follow-ups:*** *Many donations are lost simply due to a lack of follow-ups. Maintaining professional, periodic communication with potential donors is critical.*

The Future of Fundraising and Sustainability

Research suggests that only the top 10-20 non-profits in India will survive in the long run. To ensure your non-profit thrives:

- *Develop sustainability funds to support long-term operations.*

- *Reduce dependency on foreign funding (FCRA), which is subject to regulatory risks.*

- *Focus on cost-cutting strategies that do not compromise human capital or programme impact.*

- *Invest in learning and development for your fundraising team and other teams as well, that are crucial for growth.*

- *Expand and multiply your donor database through word-of-mouth advocacy.*

Final Thoughts

This was my moment. My 15 minutes of fame, and I am grateful for it. Fundraising is a journey filled with highs and lows. But with the right approach, persistence, and relationship-building, it can lead to incredible success.

Thank you, ladies and gentlemen, for your time and attention. I would be happy to take any questions.

Here we are! Through these pages, I have shared my experiences, some triumphant, some frustrating, some downright bizarre. They are my truths, my lessons, my memories. Your story might be different. In fact, it probably is. But if there is one thing I hope you take away from this book, it is that persistence pays off, and the willingness to do meaningful work can create ripples far beyond what we see.

I am not here to claim that my journey is the most remarkable one out there. Many have walked this path before me, and many will after. But I had an itch to share, to document, to pass on what I've learned. Because in today's world, knowledge graciously shared is a rare and valuable gift. If my words have sparked a thought, ignited a passion, or even given you a moment of recognition, then this endeavour has been worth it.

Whatever path you are on, I wish you success. May you chase your 'yes' with courage, may you never shy away from rejection, and may you find meaning in the work you do.

Do well for yourself, for those around you, and for the world you touch.

Spread the Love!

Epilogue

Fundraising is not just a job. It is not just a skill. It is a calling.

If you have made it this far, you already understand that fundraising is far more than securing just donations. It is the art of storytelling, the science of relationship-building, and the unwavering belief that every conversation holds the potential to change lives. It is relentless, exhilarating, and at times, unforgiving. But it can also be deeply fulfilling if you search for meaning.

To those considering a shift into fundraising, welcome to a world where resilience is your greatest currency. You will face rejection more than you ever imagined. You will navigate bureaucracy, scepticism, and the occasional heartbreak. But if you learn to embrace the 'No' as a stepping stone to the next 'Yes,' you will thrive.

To those already in the sector, you are the quiet architects of change. You know that behind every successful campaign, every transformational project, there are unseen struggles, last-minute pivots, and sleepless nights. And yet, you persist, because you understand that the most meaningful victories often come from the most unexpected places.

There is no blueprint for the perfect fundraiser. Some are strategists, others are storytellers, and some are relentless pursuers of opportunity. But all great fundraisers share a common thread, and that is the ability to see possibilities where others see obstacles.

As you continue this journey, I hope you remain curious, fearless, and relentless. I hope you remember that fundraising is not about asking for money but it's about inviting people to be part of something bigger than themselves.

The Secret Life of a Fundraiser is filled with lessons that hopefully no book can fully capture... yet!

But if this one has given you even a glimpse into the raw, unfiltered reality of this world, then my purpose is fulfilled.

So, dear reader, are you ready to chase the next 'Yes'?

Your Turn to Make an Impact!

Fundraising is not just about asking. It is about believing in a cause so deeply that others can't help but believe in it too. If this book has resonated with you, don't let the journey end here. Take some action, player.

If you are considering a career in fundraising, take the leap. The world needs passionate, persistent, and purpose-driven individuals. Start small, volunteer your time, or connect with professionals already working in the sector.

If you are already in fundraising, keep pushing boundaries. Innovate, build deeper relationships, and never lose sight of why you started. Share your experiences, mentor newcomers, and continue raising not just funds, but hope.

If you are a donor or supporter, know that every contribution, irrespective of the size, will fuel some change. Stay engaged, ask questions, and champion the causes that matter most to you.

Fundraising is not just a profession. It's a movement. Are you ready to be part of it?

Stay Connected

Would love to hear your thoughts, experiences, and fundraising journeys.

Connect with me on LinkedIn or drop a line at *wasifhani@live.com* to keep the conversation going.

And hey, if I don't respond right away… relax. I'm probably knee-deep at work, stuck in a Zoom loop, or emotionally recovering from a donor who said, *"Circle back next year"*. And if I don't respond *at all…* well, I'm probably just behaving like a 'Very Important Fundraiser'. *(Just kidding… rest assured, I'm emotionally intelligent enough to feel the ghost of every unanswered email haunting me at night).*

THE SECRET LIFE OF A FUNDRAISER

Until We Meet Again

About the Author

Wasif Hani is a dynamic fundraiser, relationship strategist, and storyteller with over 17 years of experience across banking, international markets, and the non-profit sector. From the high-stakes world of global finance to the emotionally charged mission  of social impact, Wasif has honed his ability to build trust, mobilise resources, and lead with purpose.

Over the years, he has led fundraising efforts, shaped high-impact donor strategies, and forged meaningful partnerships with corporates, foundations, and retail giving landscapes. His journey from cold calls and closed doors to breakthrough pitches and lasting alliances forms the emotional and strategic core of *The Secret Life of a Fundraiser*.

This book is more than a memoir. It's a bridge between the personal and professional, between persistence and empathy. Whether you work in development, sales, client relations, or community work, Wasif's reflections offer practical insights and emotional depth on what it takes to secure a "Yes" in a world full of "No's."

Outside of fundraising, Wasif is a passionate public speaker, emcee, and mentor. He actively advocates for ethical practices and transparency in the social sector and is committed to nurturing the next generation of fundraisers.

Connect with Wasif Hani

LinkedIn: https://www.linkedin.com/in/wasif-hani-82349718/

YouTube: Curtain Call with Wasif

Instagram: @ccwithwasif